# THE ten

## COMMANDMENTS

*of Health & Wellness*

# PAULA WHITE

THE

# ten

## COMMANDMENTS

*of Health & Wellness*

# WITH DODD ROMERO

It is always important to consult your physician before starting an exercise program if any of the following apply to you:

- You have chest, pain, and/or arm pain.
- You have shortness of breath.
- You have a diagnosed heart condition.
- You have joint and/or bone problems.
- You are currently taking cardiac and/or blood pressure medications.
- You have dizziness.
- You have not been physically active for a while or ever.

In most cases, people who have been moderately active and who do not have the symptoms above may start an exercise program gradually and sensibly. However, if you have any of these symptoms as you begin an exercise program, contact your physician immediately. An exercise stress test may be used to help plan your exercise program.

The information in this book does not substitute for advice or information given by your physician. You should contact your physician for advice if you have a long-term medical condition that has dietary or exercise restrictions.

THE ten COMMANDMENTS of Health & Wellness

ISBN 978-0-976058-1-9

Published by Paula White Enterprises

Paula White Ministries
P.O. Box 25151
Tampa, Florida 33622

You can reach Paula White Ministries on the Internet at www.paulawhite.org.

Cover/interior design by Koechel Peterson & Associates, Inc., Minneapolis, Minnesota.

# Contents

## About the Authors

**PAULA WHITE**, pastor, teacher, and speaker, is known for her dynamic Bible teaching with delivery as an exhorter and motivator. She is also the host of the nationally syndicated program *Paula Today* seen on TBN, BET, Church Channel, WORD Network, Court TV, Miracle Network, DayStar, CMT, INSP, SPIKE, OXYGEN, as well as many other stations. With a message that crosses denominational, cultural, and economic barriers, this mother, administrator, humanitarian, and evangelist is also the Senior Pastor of Without Walls International Church—a thriving, multiracial congregation of some 24,000 in Tampa, Florida, one of the fastest growing churches in the country.

**DODD ROMERO**, owner of Bod By Dodd, Inc., is widely regarded by many in the sports and entertainment industries as the best physical and mental conditioning expert in the world. He does this by combining the spiritual and physical beings as one. His long list of clients include such greats as Denzel Washington, Lenny Kravitz, Brian Grant, Alex Rodriguez (A-Rod), and Pastor Paula White. And for the first time, he is offering his formula to anyone who wants to go to the next level to be the best that God created them to be.

# Dedication

For several years it has been my heartfelt desire to release a book on the principles of health and wellness—principles that are foundational in my life, and I pray in yours as well.

God has given us biblical principles to govern and guide us in every area of our lives. In 1 Corinthians our bodies are described as the temples of God here on this earth (3:16–17), which should be used to glorify God (6:19–20). Taking care of our temple should be a priority in our lives.

God wants to see you whole—whole in spirit, soul, *and* body—so you can walk out your purpose and destiny…and be at your best mentally, spiritually and *physically*, to achieve the life He has designed for you.

It's my privilege and honor to collaborate with my friend Dodd Romero, a leading expert in the world of physical and mental conditioning. He's been such a blessing in my life, helping me to prepare myself to do all the tasks the Lord has asked me to do.

It's my prayer that as you read and apply the principles found in *The 10 Commandments of Health and Wellness*, you will incorporate them as a vital part of your everyday life, in order to be all that God has intended you to be!

I thank my heavenly Father for giving me this opportunity to share these physical and spiritual principles with you. As you learn ways to prioritize healthier eating and nutrition habits, add exercise and stress-reducing techniques into your schedule, reap the benefits of fasting, and daily meditate on and implement spiritual principles, I know they will help you fulfill your God-given assignment—whether in your career or business, as a parent or spouse, as a fitness enthusiast or athlete, and in your personal, everyday life!

Lastly, I dedicate this book to you, my friend—and in reading *The 10 Commandments of Health and Wellness*, I pray you will take these principles and make them a part of living your life as the temple of God—by His Grand Design.

God bless you.

*Paula*

Paula White

## Dedication

I would like to dedicate this book to my father, Ray Romero, who taught me by his example the value of an extreme work ethic, discipline, and what a real man of honor is.

And to my mother, Jody Romero, for instilling the principle that adversity comes into our lives to make us stronger. I grew up hearing her say, "Son, remember the same fire that melts butter makes steel stronger."

And to my sister, Kippie Maespohl, who to this day I have never heard say a curse word, for giving me a living example of a woman filled with the Holy Spirit.

And to my little brother, Stan Romero, who is not so little anymore but will always be my little brother in my heart and soul. I want to thank you for inspiring me the most. I always knew you believed in me, and I always wanted to prove you right.

And last, but certainly not least, to my girls—my wife, Sabina, and my daughter, Gianna—for being my soldiers in any battle I fight and for being there to fight beside me every step of the way. I couldn't have a more supportive family.

Thank you, Jesus.

Dodd Romero

# THE WAY
## *God Looks*
# AT HEALTH

### *by Paula White*

**H**ave you ever been to a circus and seen one of the performers balance several spinning plates on sticks that were held by that performer's hands and mouth? Have you ever watched a juggler at work juggling five or more objects?

Both tricks can be sustained for a few minutes. But we'd all decide rather quickly, wouldn't we... "that's no way to live 24/7!"

Even so, that's the way many of us *are* living in today's world.

We are juggling too many balls. We are trying our best to keep too many plates spinning.

Even if we don't *want* to live a juggling, plate-spinning

life, we live in a world that is continually pulling at us to specialize and compartmentalize. Gone are the days of general stores. We shop at specialty stores or at large stores that have "departments." Gone are the days of family doctors—today any one family might have an internist, a pediatrician, a surgeon, a dermatologist, a cardiologist, a gynecologist, and other specialty doctors on speed dial. In our higher education system, we usually earn a degree in a specialty area, and then we pursue a career that makes us an expert in a fairly narrow profession or field of expertise.

In our personal lives, we tend to take on various roles and shift from one to the next almost hourly at times—we function as spouse, parent, worker, friend, chauffeur, errand runner, club member, Christian worker, leader, follower, and so forth and so on. We divide our lives into what is mental, emotional, physical, and spiritual. We worship God on Sundays and pursue secular success Monday through Saturday. We work hard during certain hours, so we can play hard during other hours.

Our lives end up being fragmented and disoriented.

In many cases, fragmentation and disorientation lead to frustration, stress, discouragement, and a loss of identity. And too often, over time our fragmentation and frayed identity contribute to very poor health. Disease can also be stated as "dis-ease." Something about our being is out of harmony and out of sync.

God's way is one hundred percent opposite of man's way.

God sees ALL of a person. He doesn't fragment us, divide us, or compartmentalize us. He sees a person as a whole human being.

God sees every area of your life as functioning together—He sees us an expression of His creativity that is totally unique, totally balanced, completely interrelated and unified, and fully functioning.

God calls us as human beings to pursue wholeness and to see ourselves as He sees us.

**Three Important Truths.** There are three things I have learned through the years that are very important for me to share with you at the beginning of this book.

*First, you are responsible for setting priorities and establishing the habits of your own life.* What you believe to be important will determine how you spend your time and energy. What you believe about your value to God and your value to other people will determine your habits. I challenge you to take responsibility for your health. Even if your spouse refuses to keep the 10 Commandments of Health and Wellness presented in this book, you can keep them for yourself. Choose to do so.

*Second, God has an overall set of principles that produce the best possible health for each person.* We call these principles "commandments" in this book because the consequences associated with these principles are very similar to the consequences associated with the commandments in God's Word. If a person keeps these commandments, that person experiences greater health. If a person disobeys these commandments, poorer health is likely the result.

*Third, God does not separate the spiritual you and the physical you.* Your inner and outer being are like the two sides of the same coin. They are ways of expressing the same YOU. My coauthor in this book is Dodd Romero. I met Dodd a couple of years ago shortly after I had made a decision that I was going to be as good as I could possibly be in EVERY area of my life, balanced and whole. Dodd is a personal trainer and a brother in Christ. He knows how to perfect the physical body—through sound nutritional principles, health practices, and conditioning exercises—better than any person I've ever met. And he practices what he preaches. For years he has held the title "The Fittest Man in America."

The more Dodd and I worked together, and the more we shared the Word of God with each other, the more we both came to the same conclusion: Every principle or "commandment" that leads to good physical health has a strong spiritual counterpart. And vice versa. The principles of good spiritual health can be applied to a person's physical being. This book is our attempt to put the physical and the spiritual together. Dodd presents the physical concepts associated with each commandment, and I present the spiritual concepts.

**God Is the Author of All Health.** Please understand also at the outset of this book that I am a firm believer in divine health and divine healing. At times God uses prayer as a catalyst for His healing power. At other times God uses medicines and medical procedures as tools for His healing power. All healing, however, ultimately comes from God.

I also know that, even though I am a woman who has great faith in God and who believes wholeheartedly in healing miracles, I have been sick at times—and many of those times, the sickness was not the devil's doing. I became ill because of the way I treated, or mistreated, my own body. I didn't intentionally do harm to myself or intentionally use any substance that was harmful. Not at all! What I did was fail to do what was *healthful* for my body. I failed to treat my body with full respect and failed to give my body all that it needed to stay healthy. In other words, I didn't take *care* of my physical temple in the way I knew I should.

I had no excuses.

In my teen years, I was a competitive gymnast at a world-class level. I know what it means to be an athlete. I know what it takes to stay strong. Even so, there was a time in my life when I allowed myself to become so overbooked and overextended in ministry events and activities that I became physically exhausted and, in the process, became deathly ill.

Every person has a physical area of weakness, and my area of weakness seems to be my lungs. That's somewhat ironic, isn't it? The very gift I have for preaching and teaching involves lung power, and it is my lungs that can also be my weakest physical organ. I developed such severe lung problems at one point that my lungs would drastically drop in their ability to function. Through a very strong combination of faith-filled prayer, rest, and medical help, I regained the health of my lungs. In the process, I made a decision:

*The busier my schedule and the greater*
*the challenges God places before me,*
*the more I must pay attention to my physical health*
*and pursue both spiritual and physical wholeness.*

Doesn't that ring true for you in your life? The more you have to do, the more disciplined you need to be in leading a balanced life filled with all of the good things that contribute to energy, strength, stamina, and health. Life is a gift. If you continually violate the principles of God for sustaining that gift of life, you will ultimately compromise your health and well-being.

I lead one of the busiest travel and work schedules of any person I know. I also take the time necessary to stay healthy so I can keep that schedule. I work out regularly. I eat the right things to fuel my body. I try to get sufficient sleep. I take time to rest and play. I spend long hours in prayer, in study of God's Word, and in reflection about how to apply God's Word to practical living. I am in active, ardent pursuit of wholeness.

I've learned that taking care of my physical body does *not* mean that I take less care of my spiritual being. It does *not* mean that I neglect basic obligations and responsibilities I have to other people. It *does* mean that I have had to make some decisions about my schedule, and I have had to cut out some activities and make certain choices so I can pursue good health habits consistently.

The end result, however, is worth any sacrifice of temporary and superficial activities. The end result is a greater vibrancy of living, a higher quality of life, and greater joy. The end result is health, energy, and strength.

**The Choice.** Each of us faces a choice. The truth is…God wants you to be whole.

Do you want for yourself what God wants for you?

# THE ten COMMANDMENTS

*of Health & Wellness*

## WHY I KNOW THE
## *Physical & Spiritual*
## BELONG TOGETHER

### *by Dodd Romero*

I have worked as a physical trainer for more than twenty years. My first "clients" were fellow high school students who admired my level of fitness and wanted to learn from me how to get stronger so they could be more successful at sports. I was eager to share what I knew. I'm still eager to share!

Through the years, I've learned a great deal about what it takes to have the maximum physical energy and strength possible. I've also learned a great deal about sickness.

My daughter, Gianna, was born with an inability to metabolize proteins fully. Her condition was rare and continually life-threatening. For the first four years of her life, my wife, Sabina, and I seemed to spend as much time at hospitals and clinics as we did at work and at home. We learned more about how the medical world functions than we ever cared to know. I have tremendous respect and admiration for the medical professionals who worked with us, but I also know their limitations. Doctors do not heal. They can be instruments used by God, but only God heals.

When Gianna was four years old, she developed severe liver problems that resulted in very high ammonia levels in her brain. Her physicians did not believe she would survive, and if she did survive, they predicted she would have severe brain damage. She needed a liver transplant, and the possibility of finding a suitable donated liver seemed extremely remote, especially as rapidly as she was slipping toward death.

It was at that time that I got very serious about God.

From the time I was a boy, I have had a sensitive heart toward God and have loved God. My father especially had a tremendous influence on me and taught me to use my physical strength for gentle purposes. He was the one who, in a quiet and loving way, taught me to turn my physical gifts toward training rather than fighting. I had not, however, been very faithful for many years in praying, attending church, or walking out my faith in God. With Gianna near death in the hospital, I fell to my knees in a nearby chapel and prayed nonstop for several days not only for her healing and life, but for myself, to be forgiven and to become useful in new ways for God's work.

The day miraculously came when the physicians at the

hospital told us that a donor liver was on its way. I walked with Gianna all the way to the operating room, encouraging her to believe God and to LIVE and not die. And then, Sabina and I sat for hour upon hour, trusting God for the miracle only He could do.

Believe me, our faith was high for a miracle!

I knew deep in my heart that God was at work. One way I knew that was because of the surgeon who had agreed to do the transplant operation. Not only was this man the foremost liver-transplant surgeon in the entire world—who just happened to be affiliated with the hospital where we were—but he was a man I had helped in previous years. This surgeon had come to me one day when I was in the hospital on a Gianna-related visit and had hit my upper arm. He spoke only one word, "Steroids?"

I replied, "No, sir. A lot of hard work."

When I responded so quickly and positively, he said, "You may be just the person to help me." This man went on to tell me that he had lost partial use of his right hand, and as a surgeon, such an impairment meant the end of his usefulness as a practicing surgeon. I began to work with him and helped him with both a nutritional and exercise program, and within a few months he had regained full use of his hand.

I was amazed that he was to be Gianna's surgeon…and yet not amazed. God's ways are always higher than our ways and beyond our expectations.

This surgeon's "assisting surgeon" was also someone I

had known in the past. When I met with this man—who is very likely the second most reputable liver-transplant surgeon in the world—I didn't recognize him at first. But he recognized me. He said, "Dodd, do you remember when I came to you one summer in high school? I wanted to be on the football team, and I offered you $1,500 if you would train me over the summer so I could be strong enough to make the team. You turned me down. I was very angry with you for turning me down."

I remembered. The truth was, this man did not have the physical stature to be a football player, no matter how much he worked out or how strong he became. He was, on the other hand, one of the smartest guys I had ever met.

The surgeon continued, "You told me to take my money and go to some kind of camp that summer that would train my mind. You told me that my mind was my greatest asset, and that's what I needed to develop."

I nodded. I remembered the moment. It hadn't been easy for me to turn down that kind of money at that time, but I knew I had told him the right thing.

He continued, "That was the summer I became interested in medicine. My desire to become a physician developed as a result of the program I pursued that summer. In an odd way, I owe you my career as a surgeon. I'm honored to do what I can to give your little girl a new start in life."

Like I said, God's ways are always higher than our ways.

Gianna not only lived through the surgery, but she thrived.

In fact, she thrived beyond all medical expectations. Less than two weeks after the surgery, she was in such excellent shape that the doctors sent her home. The liver was such a perfect match that the physicians refused to prescribe any antirejection drugs for her. She has never needed any of those drugs during the last three years. Not only did she regain her health, she experienced better health than ever before. She had a new ability to metabolize proteins. She experienced absolutely no brain damage. And she is one of the most wonderful, outgoing, loving little girls you could ever hope to meet.

God performed a miracle. He used surgeons, a family who was generous and loving enough to donate the liver of their child killed in an accident, and countless prayers from our families and friends. God is the healer, and I praise Him daily for His healing power.

During the last three years, I have become convinced again and again, in new and deeper ways, that God's principles for physical health are the same as His principles for spiritual strength. I have become equally convinced that the physical and the spiritual are intended to be so linked together that you cannot tell them apart.

When I first met Paula White, I knew that God had sent her to my life to teach me more about God's Word and more about God's presence and power. She has been my coach even as I have been her coach. I am honored that she would give me this opportunity to share with you what I know about healing and wholeness of the physical body. I am equally honored that she would be willing to link her understanding of health with mine, and that together we can present to you the 10 Commandments of Health and Wellness.

I challenge you to believe for God's highest and best in your life.

THE
# ten
COMMANDMENTS
*of Health & Wellness*

# *Commandment 1*

## BELIEVE YOU CAN
## *Experience*
## BETTER HEALTH

*"What a person believes determines
what a person does."*

COACH
DODD:

## *Believing* Is the Foundation

"Believing" may seem like an odd starting point to you as you seek to learn about and keep the 10 Commandments of Health and Wellness—but *believing* that you can experience greater health is the foundation for all successful health practices I know.

"Of course I want better health," you may be saying.

My question is not whether you *want* better health— you probably wouldn't be reading this book if you didn't *want* better health. My question is, "Do you *believe* you can experience greater health."

Through the years, I've been amazed at the number of people I've met who don't truly believe they can live a healthier life. I'm beginning to think I've heard all the excuses. Some of the most frequent statements I hear are these:

- "I just can't lose weight. I've tried every diet known to mankind, and they just don't work for me."
- "I don't have time to exercise—and besides, I get too tired when I exercise, and I have too much to do to be tired all the time."
- "I've been out of shape too long to get back in shape."
- "I inherited bad health from my parents."
- "I don't have any willpower, and getting healthier takes willpower."

I'm here to tell you that:

- You CAN lose weight.
- You CAN find time to exercise and experience greater levels of energy.
- You CAN get in shape no matter your previous experiences.
- You DO have the willpower it takes.
- Most of the factors related to health and prevention of chronic diseases and conditions are related to choices related to behavior, not to genetics.

Be encouraged!

Believe that you can and *will* experience greater health, beginning today.

## What Happens If You *Don't Believe*

Unless you truly believe that you can and will experience greater health by following God's principles, you won't take the first steps necessary to experience better health, and, even more importantly, you will give up the first moment you feel discouraged. If you feel a twinge of discomfort…a little guilt…or a slight setback, you will conclude, "This isn't for me," and quit.

Don't let it happen!

The path to better health is rarely a straight upward trend line. There are times when every person seems to hit a plateau or even take a slight step backward before going three steps forward. These are normal adjustment periods as the body seeks to create a new balance internally.

Some people become discouraged if they see a "slow-down" in their progress. They may experience great results for the first few weeks of a new health plan, but then the results aren't quite as great—for example, their *rate* of weight loss may become slower. This is normal. Too many changes made too quickly can be damaging to the body. Give your body time to adjust to change and refuse to become discouraged.

**Think:**

*I didn't get where I'm at overnight, and I won't reach perfection overnight. But today—right now—I can make a U-turn from where I'm headed to where I want to go!*

Anticipate these trends and potential "discouragers" and set your believing for the long haul. The truth for every person is this: You didn't get where you are overnight—and you won't be able to change everything you'd like to change overnight.

Start believing...and *keep believing.*

### A Seven-Week Health Program.

The program at the end of this book covers seven weeks. My hope for you is that these seven weeks will allow you time to see that this program is a *way of living.* It is far more than a get-fit or weight-loss program. Most people, however, have a little difficulty taking on the whole of their life. They find it easier to make a commitment to a shorter time frame, and that is the reason for the seven weeks. As one man said to me, "I'm not sure I can believe for a complete and lasting change, but I am sure that I can stick with a program for seven weeks." I'm believing the same will be true for you!

## Steps to Help Your *Believing*

There are three steps I encourage you to take as you begin your quest for better health:

*First, ask those closest to you to support and encourage you as you seek better health.* Get a commitment from your "inner circle"—family members and close friends—that they will neither nag you nor tempt you.

*Second, make a decision that you will not only believe that you* can *experience greater health, but also make a decision that you* can *and* will *come to enjoy the process!*

Very few programs call upon participants to *like* a program. I always challenge those who work with me to set their attitudes to *liking* the new routine. Certainly, I know that most people do not like change, and most people feel deprived of something as they begin a new health plan. But I also know that those who stick with my program come to like not only the results they are experiencing, but also the process itself.

They may have thought drinking water was boring in the past...but they come to see a cool glass of water as the most refreshing option.

They may have hated the thought of exercise in the past...but they come to enjoy a brisk walk early in the morning.

They may have found food that wasn't loaded with fat and salt to be rather bland...but they come to enjoy the real taste of whole foods to the point that too much fat or salt is unappealing.

Trust me, these changes can and do occur. And as the weeks pass, you *will* enjoy the process. Set your attitude toward enjoying the process. Refuse to complain or speak discouraging words to yourself. Instead, tell yourself repeatedly, "I *like* becoming healthier." A big part of the process in becoming healthier is to *think* like a healthy person rather than a person in need of more health.

If you haven't enjoyed fish in the past, say to yourself every time you eat fish, "I like fish."

If you haven't enjoyed exercising in the past, say to yourself every time you are exercising, "I like exercising."

"But isn't this lying to myself?" you may be saying.

No. It is speaking to yourself about an inner, still unseen "like" that exists deep within you but isn't fully visible to you yet. Trust me on this—you *are* going to like fresh, great tasting fish and heart-rate-increasing exercise more at the end of seven weeks than you presently do.

*Third, set realistic goals and time frames for reaching your goals.* One of the main reasons that "quitters" give for quitting a health program is that they felt hopeless when they saw that they weren't going to get to their goal when they thought they'd arrive. I recently heard about one person who decided she wanted to lose seventy pounds and get in shape before a high school reunion. Unfortunately, she had waited until four months before the reunion to make this decision! After a month of serious dieting and exercise, she had lost only ten pounds. Rather than rejoice that she had lost that weight, she became depressed that she wouldn't be able to lose all she had wanted to lose before the big event, and she opted for an eating binge and no exercise with the statement, "I may as well go to the party fat and happy rather than only slightly thinner and miserable."

As you set goals, talk to your trainer or physician about a time frame for reaching your goals. Be realistic, yet optimistic.

**Setting Goals.** Every person needs goals toward which he or she is working every day. Since I deal with physical training, the goals I encourage a person to make are physical goals.

Many people think that a goal is the place where you want to end up—and it is. But a goal also has a *starting point*. As part of setting a goal, you need to know where you are right now. I recommend that a person do two things:

- *Take a "Before" Photo.* Your "before" photo can be for your eyes only! Wear a swimsuit, underwear, or anything that you are comfortable wearing that shows your body honestly. Use a plain background. Take a few front shots (including a hands-on-hips photo and a "biceps flex" muscle pose in which you actually try to make your muscles "bulge"). Take a side shot. With today's digital cameras, you probably can take these photos using a timer on your camera—nobody else need ever see your "before" photo. The purpose of these photos is to motivate you and over time to give you a real sense of progress.

- *Take "Before" Measurements.* Also take measurements
  that provide a baseline. Use a flexible tape measure and
  record the inches at the GREATEST measurement:

Weight        *Day 1* _____ *After Day 49* _____

Chest         *Day 1* _____ *After Day 49* _____

Waist         *Day 1* _____ *After Day 49* _____

Hips          *Day 1* _____ *After Day 49* _____

Right Thigh   *Day 1* _____ *After Day 49* _____

Left Thigh    *Day 1* _____ *After Day 49* _____

Right Arm     *Day 1* _____ *After Day 49* _____

Left Arm      *Day 1* _____ *After Day 49* _____

If you are consulting a physician before you begin your
health program, you may also want to get some baseline
health-related numbers:

## CHOLESTEROL

Good HLD   *Day 1* _____ *After Day 49* _____

Bad LDL    *Day 1* _____ *After Day 49* _____

Total      *Day 1* _____ *After Day 49* _____

## TRIGLYCERIDES   *Day 1* _____ *After Day 49* _____
## BLOOD PRESSURE

Upper number   *Day 1* _____ *After Day 49* _____

Lower number   *Day 1* _____ *After Day 49* _____

## HEART RATE   *Day 1* _____ *After Day 49* _____

Choose a few words that describe how you feel. Write them down.

_____

_____

_____

Now, describe in a few sentences or words WHAT YOU BELIEVE can be the way you will feel after seven weeks.

_____

_____

_____

_____

## *Faith* Comes Before Action

Faith is at the core of *everything* we ultimately do in our lives. If we believe we *can't* do something...we don't.

If we believe we *can* do something...we do!

For those of us who are Christians, faith is made more powerful by the truth that the Holy Spirit indwells us and helps us do those things that are pleasing in God's sight. Even if we don't fully believe we can do something in our own strength and ability, we are challenged by God's Word to believe that we can do it *with God's help!* The apostle Paul said, "I can do all things through Christ which strengtheneth me" (Philippians 4:13).

One of the best definitions I've ever heard of will-power for the Christian is this: Willpower is MY will and GOD's power.

When God gave the Ten Commandments to the Children of Israel, He made this the first commandment: "Thou shalt have no other gods before me" (Exodus 20:3). God was saying to His people: "Believe in Me!" The basis for keeping all the other commandments that followed was rooted in *believing God.*

No matter what good thing you desire in your life, God is the source of that good thing—He is the creator of all goodness, He is the giver of all goodness, and He is the one who enables us both to seek and to receive His goodness.

## "Your attitude determines your altitude."

The key to experiencing the fullness of God's goodness—in spirit and in body—is to *believe* with your faith that God is at work in you...through you...and all around you. He is making a way for you where there has been no way. He is doing in you what has never been done before. He is creating and re-creating your life to become a mirror image of Christ Jesus' spiritual maturity, emotional character, and physical fitness.

"But," you may be saying, "I'm not sure God really cares about my physical body or health."

Hear the truth of God to you today: God cares tremendously about your health and physical well-being. He cares about your emotional and spiritual well-being. God's Word emphasizes WHOLENESS. God wants you to live in a harmonious wellness that covers your body, mind, emotions, spirit, and all of your relationships. There's no part of your being that God leaves out. He sees you as a whole, and He moves continually to make you whole.

When Jesus encountered a sick person, He made that person *whole*. He didn't address physical issues without addressing the spiritual. Neither did He address only spiritual issues without addressing the physical. In one instance, Jesus forgave sin and commanded that a paralyzed man pick up his pallet and walk. In another instance, Jesus healed so that a person might be restored to worship with others. God doesn't divide your life into categories labeled "physical" or "spiritual." He sees you as a whole human being in need of wellness in every area of your life.

Be assured today: God *will* help you have greater health as you trust in Him and then obey what He has commanded.

## 3 Insights into *Believing...*

Let me share these three aspects of *believing* God's Word as you begin your new health program that connects the physical and spiritual.

*First, believe what God's Word says about you: "You are His temple on this earth."* The Bible tells us, "Know ye not that ye are the temple of God, and that the Spirit of God dwelleth in you? If any man defile the temple of God, him shall God destroy; for the temple of God is holy, which temple ye are" (1 Corinthians 3:16–17).

God's Holy Spirit resides within you if you have accepted Jesus as your Savior. Jesus said He would send the Holy Spirit to live within every person who believes in Him as the Son of God. Your body as a Christian, therefore, is a vessel— or in Paul's writings to the Corinthians, a *temple*—in which the Holy Spirit dwells.

If you had invited Jesus to your home, and you knew with certainty that He was coming this afternoon, you probably would have done everything possible to make sure your home was as clean and beautiful as possible. This is the challenge God gives us in His Word about our bodies. He challenges us to see ourselves as the "home on this earth" that the Holy Spirit calls His own. We must keep His home as pollution-free, clean, and beautiful as possible. We must seek to have all the energy necessary to fulfill what the Holy Spirit calls us to do. We must seek to honor the Holy Spirit in all aspects of our behavior. And ultimately, we must seek to bring glory to God by the way we live, which includes the way we treat our physical bodies.

I invite you to make a new commitment to God and to yourself today:

*I will treat my body as the temple of the Holy Spirit.*

*Second, start where you are. Believe for the first step!* Jesus never discounted a person's faith. In fact, He said that even a little faith could accomplish much! He taught His followers, "If ye have faith as a grain of mustard seed, ye shall say unto this mountain, Remove hence to yonder place; and it shall remove; and nothing shall be impossible unto you" (Matthew 17:20).

A grain of mustard seed of the variety that grows in Israel is so small it is barely visible—it is like a grain of finely ground pepper. A mountain, on the other hand, is the largest physical object that a person could see in Jesus' day. Jesus was telling His disciples, "Even if you only have the least amount of faith...you can accomplish the most!"

God's Word tells us that we each have been given a "measure" of faith (Romans 12:3). That means you have at least a mustard grain's amount of faith with which to believe God for better health. Plant that seed into the things that are presented in this book—use your little bit of faith to believe that as you obey the rest of the Commandments of Health and Wellness, you *will* see results.

*Say to yourself often in any given day as you work through the seven weeks of this plan: "I can do ALL things through Christ which strengtheneth me!"*

You may not be able to believe fully right now for the big picture goal of the health you'd like to have. But...I am convinced that you can believe for the first step toward that goal. You can get up tomorrow morning, lace on your walking shoes, and go out for a fifteen-minute walk. You can make a choice to have a good breakfast rather than a bad breakfast or no breakfast. You can plan your day to include a time of quiet and prayer. I know you can! Believe you can...and you will.

*Third, ask God to help you.* Don't just "think" about asking. Ask! Verbalize your prayer—in other words, pray out loud. Be bold in asking God for help as you seek to do what you know is good for you to do! God's Word says that we have not because we ask not (James 4:2). Ask God today to help you believe for better health. Ask God today to help you do the things necessary for experiencing better health. Ask God today to encourage you when you feel discouraged and to give you wisdom in areas where you may be lacking wisdom. Trust the Holy Spirit to be your helper!

*Believe that TODAY is the day*
*to begin a new health plan that*
*not only can but WILL result*
*in better health for the*
*WHOLE*
*of your life!*

THE
# ten
COMMANDMENTS
*of Health & Wellness*

# Commandment 2

## TOSS OUT THE
## *Tempters*

*"Get rid of everything that
doesn't produce good in your life."*

## Clear Out *the Bad* to Make Room for *the Good*

Temptation is a powerful force. That's true in every person's physical life as well as spiritual life.

Most physical temptations are a matter of habit. We have become accustomed to an old pattern of living—generally one that didn't produce the best health possible. We are stuck in the rut of that old pattern, and if we encounter any changes that are difficult, we are tempted to revert to what we once knew or once did. Changing your level of health is largely a matter of trading in old bad habits for new good habits.

Some of those habits are related to the way you eat and drink. Some are related to the way you move physically—or exercise. Some are related to the way you sleep and get rid of stress. Some are related to habits rooted in your attitude and thinking.

The good news is that if you have had the ability to develop a bad habit, you have the ability to develop a good one to take its place. It is true for most vehicles on most roads, and it is true for most people on life's highway: You can make a U-turn!

As you deal with tempters in your life, be aware that no person is ever beyond temptation. Never think that you are too old to be tempted. Never think that you can become so healthy that you are immune from all disease or that you can become so fit that you are immune from injury. Seeking and living in good health takes constant awareness and diligence. This does not mean that gaining and maintaining good health is difficult or impossible—it *does* mean that good health should never be taken for granted. Seeking and maintaining good health requires ongoing choice-making, and the good news is that once habits related to good health are established, making those choices becomes easier and easier. Never assume, however, that you are beyond being "tripped up" by a temptation.

*Changing your level of health is largely a matter of trading in old bad habits for new good habits.*

Also be aware that every person has unique temptations. What is tempting to you may not be at all tempting to me. Know your own areas of weakness and guard against them. If you know that there's a broken place in your backyard fence, you don't ignore it. You rebuild the fence. The same is true when it comes to what tempts you. If you know something is a temptation, you can and should take very positive steps toward avoiding that temptation or building up your defenses against it.

Through the last twenty-five years, I've worked as a professional trainer and learned two important principles related to temptation:

One, you can't eat what you don't first purchase and have available to eat.

Two, you CAN choose to turn off as many negative "cues" as possible.

There are very practical ways in which you can act on both of these principles.

## Four *Practical Steps* to Turning Off *Temptation*

You can take each of these steps toward better health starting *today*:

*First, don't go to the grocery store without a list.* Determine that you are only going to purchase what you have *planned in advance* to purchase. For the most part, you'll find the healthiest foods on the outer walls of the grocery store. That's where the fresh fruit and vegetables, fish and poultry, and milk products tend to be.

*Second, clear out your pantry, cupboards, and your refrigerator.* Remove all foods that do not contribute to good health. If you are in doubt, check the label on a food item. If you find words that you can't readily pronounce, you are likely dealing with an additive, preservative, or some form of chemical that—over time and in sufficient quantity—can do your body more harm than good. If you find the words *transfat, hydrogenated fat, partially hydrogenated fat,* or any other word used to hide harmful fats in a product, toss the item. This means, by the way, that most bakery-style goods, such as cookies, cupcakes, cake mixes, most "snack foods" (including chips), and many breads, need to hit the trash.

Also remove all products that have refined sugar in them. Be aware that sugar is sometimes labeled sucrose, fructose, lactose, and in other ways. Sugar accelerates the aging process, and it often leads to Type II diabetes and elevated cholesterol levels. It has been linked to behavioral disorders, and it is addictive. Are you aware that a twelve-ounce can of carbonated soda has between eight and ten teaspoons of sugar? That's more refined sugar than a person should have in a year!

Remove products made with refined white flour and products that are heavily laced with salt (labeled sodium).

*Third, don't eat a meal you haven't THOUGHT about in advance.* We all live busy, stressful lives, and very often we eat foods "on the run." The result is that we eat whatever is closest or easiest to purchase. Give thought to what you are going to put into your body as fuel. As much as possible, prepare foods in advance for quick assembly at mealtime—chop up fruit and keep a large bowl of fruit in your refrigerator; chop up vegetables to make a quick salad or stir-fry dish; precook poultry and debone it so you have meat readily available to add to a salad or to add to a plate of steamed vegetables. Take your lunch to work. If you've already thought about a meal in advance, chances are that you won't be nearly as susceptible to sudden urges to eat or to tempting aromas.

If you eat out at a restaurant, plan before you walk in the door of that restaurant what you are going to have. If at all possible, don't even open the menu to read it. Be quick to ask for your poultry or fish to be grilled, your vegetables steamed lightly, and your salad with no dressing (olive oil and vinegar on the side).

*Fourth, eat several small portions of food a day.* People who eat five to six small portions of food evenly spaced through-out a day generally find it easier to lose weight and maintain their weight at an optimal level. They have fewer tempta-tions to binge eat or to eat the wrong foods. They have more energy and sleep better at night. The foremost reason is that their blood sugar levels are kept more even, with fewer highs and lows that trigger hunger and fatigue.

Each small meal needs to include a balance of protein and carbohydrates. These small meals need to be taken into the body every three to four hours. The last meal should be consumed at least two hours before bedtime. (There's more on balancing protein and carbohydrates later in this book.)

## Winning the Battle of *the Mind*

A woman once said to me, "Every time I diet I become much more aware of every food commercial on television and every billboard for food on the roads!" The truth is, it was likely a steady bombardment of those commercials and billboards that contributed to her becoming overweight in the first place.

Another person said to me, "The first couple of weeks of my new health plan, I thought about food all the time!" That can be the case.

Here are a couple of suggestions for handling the men-tal battle related to temptations.

*First, turn off your television set for the first three weeks of this plan.* If you have a favorite program you don't want to miss, record the program and fast-forward through the com-mercials.

*Second, keep your eyes on the road.* Some people find it helpful to listen to audio tapes as they drive. This tends to absorb the attention they might normally give to billboards and restaurant signs. (As you might suspect, I often recommend teaching CDs by Paula White!)

*Third, if your imagination is snared by the temptation of a particular food item, take action immediately.* Don't allow yourself to dwell on the idea! Immediately say, "I'm not going to eat that today. I have more control over my life than to give in to the message of a commercial or billboard." And then choose to think about something else that *demands your concentration*—perhaps a problem you are sorting out related to your work or to a creative project that you are pursuing. I know one person who begins to quote scriptures when she feels tempted to eat or to skip her appointment at the gym.

## *Planning* Tackles Temptation Head-on

You may be saying, "All this planning and thinking in advance about food—doesn't that increase the temptation to eat?" The exact opposite is nearly always true.

If you plan in advance, you send a signal to your brain, "Brain, you no longer need to think continually about food. The decisions about food have already been made!" Planning in advance also allows you to eat in advance of powerful hunger urges.

If you can imagine "hunger" as being on a scale of one to ten, try to eat when your hunger level is between four and six. If you eat before then, you never really feel hunger, and, therefore, you don't have as much satisfaction from having eaten. You are likely to overeat, even in your smaller more frequent portions. If you eat after stage six, you'll be ravenous and prone to temptation. Get in touch with your own body and own feelings of hunger. *Know* when you are at hunger levels four to six!

Until you get fully in touch with your own hunger levels, eat by the clock. Generally speaking, hunger comes every three to four hours after your previous meal, whether that meal was large or small. Plan in advance to eat at that interval—in many ways, you'll be "preempting" bad decisions regarding food.

Planning covers other areas of your new health plan, not only food. We cover this in the next chapter more thoroughly, but the point to make here is this: You must become intentional about *all* areas of your health and well-being.

What tempts you to stay up late and, therefore, fail to get sufficient sleep?

What tempts you to stay away from the gym?

What tempts you to cancel your daily walk with a friend?

What tempts you to skip church or Bible study?

Face up to all the areas in which you now are frequently tempted. The way beyond most of those temptations is to PLAN for a healthful alternative in advance! Just as you choose the best route to save time as you travel across your city or across the nation, choose the best route to health. Choose a route that bypasses as many temptations as possible.

## Off with *the Old*, On to *the New!*

The very heart of repentance is this: Turn away from what is evil and negative and turn toward what is good and positive. In church language, we say, "Turn away from sin and toward godliness." Turn away from the devil and turn toward God. In the context of this book, both Dodd and I are encouraging you to turn away from all things that contribute to bad health and turn toward all things that contribute to good health.

Turning away from what is bad for you is an act of your will. The good news in this is that God said you CAN use your will to make good choices. As a Christian, you are no longer bound by your old sin nature that automatically drove you to sin. You can make choices for what is right, and the Holy Spirit will help you act on those choices and *do* what is right.

The Bible has numerous examples related to both our ability to make these choices, and God's command to make them:

- "He may know to refuse the evil, and choose the good" (Isaiah 7:15).
- "Choose you this day whom you will serve" (Joshua 24:15).
- "Let the wicked forsake his way, and the unrighteous man his thoughts: and let him return unto the LORD,

and he will have mercy upon him; and to our God, for he will abundantly pardon" (Isaiah 55:7).

- "Put off concerning the former conversation the old man, which is corrupt according to the deceitful lusts; and be renewed in the spirit of your mind; and that ye put on the new man, which after God is created in righteousness and true holiness" (Ephesians 4:22–24).

- "Walk as children of light…have no fellowship with the unfruitful works of darkness, but rather reprove them" (Ephesians 5:8, 11).

In giving the Ten Commandments to the Israelites, the second command was this: "Thou shalt not make unto thee any graven image, or any likeness of anything that is in heaven above, or that is in the earth beneath, or that is in the water under the earth: Thou shalt not bow down thyself to them, nor serve them" (Exodus 20:4–5). We tend to think of idols as little clay or metal figurines used in religious ceremonies. The word *idol* actually refers to an attitude of the heart. An idol is anything that a person greatly or fanatically desires and pursues. That puts just about everything we categorize as "addictive" in the category of an idol.

Some people wake up thinking about their first alcoholic drink, first hit of a drug, or first pill of medication—they greatly and fanatically desire and pursue that substance to make them feel good.

Some people wake up thinking about food and go to

bed at night still dreaming of the foods they wished they could have eaten during the day. They are greatly and fanatically in pursuit of food.

Some people wouldn't dream of missing a favorite television show—even with an immoral story line—or ever consider turning down an invitation from a particular person, even though they know that person likely will want them to go to a place they shouldn't go or do something they know they shouldn't do.

*God calls us at all times and in all situations to discern good from evil, and then to choose what is good.*

We tend to be people who are ruled by our own whims, fantasies, and emotions of the moment. God calls us to a saner, more beneficial way of living. He says to us, "Come, let us reason together." He calls us to discern good from evil and then to choose good.

## Overcoming the Tempter with *the Word*

One of the names for the devil in the New Testament is "tempter." Jesus had a showdown with the tempter immediately after His public baptism and the start of His ministry on this earth. I have no doubt that the tempter comes in special ways to those who decide to make a positive change—and especially those who decide to embark on a new path of doing what is right in God's eyes. This may very well include your decision to pursue a new health plan for your life. The devil never wants what is good for us. His temptation always is to get us to choose something that may *feel* good in the short run, but which will have devastating consequences in the long run.

The devil has no ability to tell "the whole truth and nothing but the truth." His temptations always include a lie or deception. His appeal is to the carnal man. A carnal-minded man does not mean you are not in relationship with God through His Son Jesus. It means you walk in the order of the natural man or are governed by your sensory perception or five senses. This is how Eve was tempted in the garden (Genesis 3). When the serpent came and enticed her, notice what happened: (1) She talked to the serpent, (2) she saw the fruit, and it looked good, (3) she touched the fruit, (4) she tasted the fruit, and (5) she smelled the fruit as she was eating it. It brought forth a death in her life. The tempter desires to do the same with us. Romans 8:6 reminds us that "to be carnally minded" or to walk in the order of being governed and ruled by sensory perception is "death" (one translation reads "deadly").

The devil will not tell you that overeating an extra pint of ice cream this month will add a pound of weight to your body…and if you continue, it will eventually be "deadly" to your overall health and well-being. He'll only entice you with messages about how good that ice cream is going to taste in the moment you are eating it.

The devil or tempter will not tell you that leading a sedentary life with no exercise can result in poor muscle tone, lower endurance, and less energy—and ultimately make you less effective in whatever work and ministry God has called you to do. The devil will only speak to you about how good it feels to "sit down and relax a little." While all things should be in moderation and balance to benefit you, this is not usually the case. There is a time for physical exertion, and there is a time for relaxation.

## "Failing to prepare is preparing to fail."

The devil will not tell you that for some people having a couple of drinks with dinner can eventually lead to alcoholism...or that overly flirtatious behavior just for the "fun of it" can lead to an affair and the demise of a marriage...or that a lifestyle of deception and dishonesty can lead to a jail sentence. He will only tell you that a drink might help you *feel* more social, a flirtation might add a few *feelings* of excitement to your boring life, and a little dishonesty might help you *feel* better about yourself and your ability to overcome a tough spot you are in. We must always ask questions about anything that seems too easy, too quick, too good to be true, or holds out the promise of too much return for too little invested. We need to ask, "Where *might* this end up?"

Things that seem too easy...nearly always require a redo.

Things that seem too good to be true...usually are.

Things that seem to yield too much return for too little investment...are usually illegal!

How did Jesus deal with the tempter? Three times, the Bible tells us, the devil came to Jesus with a temptation. Three times, Jesus replied by quoting the Word of God to the devil. Jesus confronted the devil's lies with the truth of God's Word and with the truth of Himself.

That's the way we confront the devil's temptations, too!

*First, resist.* God's Word promises us that if we resist the devil, he must flee from us (James 4:7). Therefore, the first and easiest line of defense is to say as Jesus said, "Get thee hence!" (See Matthew 4:10.) Or in today's language, "Get outta here. Leave me alone. Let go and get away!"

*Second, speak Truth.* If the temptation persists, tell the tempter who you are, in Whom you believe, and where you are headed. Remind the devil that you belong to God and that Jesus Christ is your Savior and Lord. Remind him that the Holy Spirit is your comforter, counselor, and powerful helper in all things. Remind the tempter that you are destined for wholeness. Remind the devil that he is a liar.

*Third, take positive action.* To seal your resistance against temptation, get busy doing the things that you know are good in God's eyes. Walk away from the tempting situation and walk toward the ministry opportunity God has for you. As a friend of mine said, "Any time I am tempted to get off my diet, I volunteer for an extra hour of helping in the food line at the homeless shelter." Another person once said to me, "When I get tempted to hook up with the wrong people, I head for the nursery at church and wrap my arms around a baby who needs my love and care. That keeps me embracing a person who is good for me, and keeps me out of the arms of someone who is bad for me!"

The Bible tells us that Jesus was "led up into the wilderness" by the Spirit…and the underlying truth is that the Spirit was with Jesus the entire time, enabling and empowering Him to respond the way He did. Don't think you can go it alone one-on-one with the devil. Ask the Holy Spirit to *empower* you to resist, to speak, and to act in ways that defeat the tempter in your life. Pray in Jesus' Name. Rely upon God to help you at every turn.

> *Before a builder builds, he clears the land.*
> *The same is true for us as we seek to build*
> *a life of GOOD HEALTH.*
> *Let's clear away all things that might be*
> *contributing to poor health.*

# Commandment 3

## STOCK UP WITH THE
## *Good Stuff*

*"Fill your life and your home with those
things that promote better health."*

COACH
DODD:

## Putting *Your Focus* on What Contributes to *Health*

Most people who drive automobiles know exactly what type of fuel their particular automobile uses. Occasionally a tank of the wrong octane can be tolerated, but for the most part a vehicle runs best when it has the right fuel. The same is true for our human bodies. In many ways the body is very forgiving— after all, cuts and broken bones heal, bruises disappear, and most people survive most viral and bacterial diseases they experience. Overall, however, it is very important for you to put the right fuel into your body and the right information into your mind and heart at all times.

In the pages that follow, you will find the Approved Foods list that I give to my clients. Not only will you find a list of "what" to eat, but the portion size recommended at any given "mealtime." Where appropriate, I've made recommendations about how often in any given week a food should be included in your health plan.

As a general rule, I encourage you to think in terms of "whole foods." Whole foods are those that have nothing done to them—nothing added in the way of fillers, preservatives, or added fat, salt, or sugar. Whole foods include whole pieces of fruit and vegetables as well as whole grains. Vegetables are best eaten raw or lightly steamed. Fruit is best eaten fresh, but, if necessary, choose frozen fruit over canned fruit. (Canned fruit usually has syrup with it, which has sugar.)

Meat—whether poultry or beef—should be the leanest cut possible, with all fat trimmed away. If preparing chicken, remove all skin.

I've also included a list of approved "snack items"—these may be considered small meals between the regular breakfast, lunch, and dinner mealtimes. And you'll find a list of approved beverages. You will notice that alcoholic beverages are not included on this list. There are far more downsides to consuming alcohol than there are positive benefits—in fact, any of the positive antioxidant benefits attributed to wine can be acquired in other ways.

*Fuel your body with the right foods and beverages for maximum performance— maximum strength, maximum energy, and maximum health.*

Finally, you'll find a list of approved condiments. I am a strong voice for "good foods" tasting good! At the back of this book, you'll find recipes related to some of the items on these lists.

Stock up your shelves with the right stuff. And then enjoy eating the right stuff. As I indicated earlier, you may find it easier to eat the right foods if you prepare some items in advance and have them readily available—such as a large bowl of fruit salad or the chopped-up ingredients for a healthy vegetable salad stored in sealed containers in your refrigerator.

| Approved Food | Quantity Per Mealtime | Other Notes |
|---|---|---|
| **PROTEINS** | | |
| *Poultry:* | | |
| Whole turkey breast | 7 oz | |
| Ground turkey breast | 7 oz | 99% fat free |
| Chicken breast | 7 oz | |
| Canned chicken or turkey | 7 oz | white meat |
| *Red Meat:* | | |
| Buffalo | 10 oz | LIMIT red |
| Lean beef | 10 oz | meat to no |
| Flank steak | 10 oz | more than 2 |
| Top round steak | 10 oz | times a week |
| Top sirloin | 10 oz | |
| *Fish:* | | |
| Any white-meat fish | 12 oz | |
| Tuna | 12 oz | |
| Salmon | 12 oz | |
| Canned tuna | 12 oz | in water |
| *Milk products and eggs:* | | |
| Cottage cheese | 7 oz | low-fat |
| Egg whites | 2–5 | |
| *Other:* | | |
| Whey protein shake (or powder) | 30 grams whey protein | |
| Protein bar | one | |
| Soy protein powder | 30 grams | |

| Approved Food | Quantity Per Mealtime | Other Notes |
|---|---|---|
| Protein pudding | one | |
| Protein cake | one piece | see recipe |
| Protein cupcake | one | see recipe |

## COMPLEX CARBOHYDRATES

| | | |
|---|---|---|
| All vegetables *except* carrots, peas, and corn | $1/2$ cup | |
| Sweet potato | $1/2$ | |
| Yam | $1/2$ | |
| Beans | $1/2$ cup | |
| Barley | $1/2$ cup | |
| Brown or wild rice | $1/2$ cup | steamed |
| Yucca | $1/2$ | |
| Cream of rice/cream of wheat | $1/2$ cup | cooked |
| Butternut squash | $1/2$ cup | |
| Plain brown rice cakes | two | |
| Ezekiel bread | two pieces | |
| Ezekiel wraps | two | |
| Quinoa | $1/2$ cup | |
| Whole wheat pasta | 1 cup | |

*These cereals may replace complex carbs in the health plan, serving size of 1 cup:

All Bran, Kashi, Muesli, Fibre One, Shredded Wheat,

Uncle Sam, Wheatabix, Puffed Rice, Puffed Wheat

| Approved Food | Quantity Per Mealtime | Other Notes |
| --- | --- | --- |

## FRUITS

*Fruits can be substituted for a complex carbohydrate in the health plan:

| Approved Food | Quantity Per Mealtime | Other Notes |
| --- | --- | --- |
| Acai or goji berries | 1/4 cup | |
| Apple | one | |
| Apricot | one | |
| Blackberries | 1 cup | |
| Blueberries | 1 cup | |
| Cherries | 1 cup | |
| Cranberries | 1 cup | |
| Grapes | 1 cup | trying freezing a bunch for a refreshing treat |
| Grapefruit | one | |
| Lemon | one | |
| Lime | one | |
| Mango | one | |
| Orange | one | |
| Nectarine | one | |
| Peach | one | |
| Pear | one | |
| Plum | one | |
| Prunes | two | |
| Pineapple | 1/2 cup | |
| Rhubarb | 1/2 cup | |
| Raspberries | 1 cup | |

| Approved Food | Quantity Per Mealtime | Other Notes |
|---|---|---|
| Strawberries | 1 cup | |
| Watermelon | 1 cup | |
| Tangerine | 1 cup | |

## SNACK FOODS

| | | |
|---|---|---|
| Almonds | 21 | |
| Cashews | 21 | |
| Protein waffle | one | see recipe |
| Protein pudding | one | |
| Protein pancake | one | see recipe |
| Sugar-free popsicles | unlimited | |
| Sugar-free Jello® | unlimited | |
| Almond butter | 1 tbsp | try this on a celery stick or an apple slice |
| Protein cake | one piece | see recipe |
| Protein muffin | one | 30 grams for a snack—see recipe |
| Any non-starchy vegetable | $1/2$ cup | |
| Hummus with celery stalks | 4 pieces of celery $1/2$ cup hummus | see recipe |
| Refried bean dip | $1/2$ cup | |
| Ezekiel bread | one slice | try with Splenda® and cinnamon or 1 tbsp almond butter |

| Approved Food | Quantity Per Mealtime | Other Notes |
|---|---|---|

## BEVERAGES

Fresh, pure, unflavored water

Diet drinks and soda

Sugar-free Kool Aid, Crystal
Light; sugar-free green tea
and sugar-free lemonade

Hot tea

Plain unsweetened iced tea

Coffee (black)

Skim milk — 16 oz

Rice milk — 16 oz

Soy milk — 16 oz

Other Notes: limit your sugar-free beverages to no no more than 2 a day

## CONDIMENTS

Fresh and ground herbs — try new flavors!

Ketchup

Mustard

Sea salt

Pepper (black, red, white)

BBQ sauce — use in moderation

Salsa

Hot sauce

Butter buds — use in moderation

Sugar-free maple syrup

Splenda®

Stevia (all natural sweetener)

Nutmeg

| Approved Food | Quantity Per Mealtime | Other Notes |
| --- | --- | --- |
| Cinnamon | | |
| Balsamic vinegar | | |
| All spice | | |
| Rosemary | | |
| Basil | | |
| Oregano | | |
| Mint | | |
| Dill | | |
| Thyme | | |
| Onion powder | | |
| Garlic powder | | |
| Lemon juice | | |
| Lime juice | | |
| Olive oil | | |
| Flaxseed oil | | |

## Other Areas for *"Stocking Up"*

Eating right is only part of what contributes to maximum health. There are several other things you should consider as you make a new commitment to improving your physical well-being:

- *Pure water.* Find a source of pure filtered water. You may be able to buy such water in one- or five-gallon containers. Or purchase bottled water that is pure and filtered. The optimal choice, of course, is to have a water filter for the tap water in your home. The best water purification systems involve reverse osmosis or distillation. Reverse osmosis systems force water through membranes to remove minerals in the water. Distillation is the process of turning water into vapor and then condensing the vapors again into water that is free of heavy metals left behind. There are also absolute 1-micron filtration systems available that remove all particles larger than one micron in size—this means that even common parasitic protozoans are removed. Avoid drinking water that has been chlorinated.

- *Nutritional supplements.* You'll note that protein powders are on the lists above. Make sure you are using high-quality protein powder. Ask at your local nutrition store. In a later section, I'll be recommending supplements that most people are wise to take to ensure adequate total nutrition. Stock up on the items you need.

- *A cooler and plastic containers.* Get a little cooler and some plasticware containers for your use when you are on the road, at work, or away from your house. Make sure you have plenty of pure water and recommended foods with you to help you withstand temptations.

- *Air filters.* Change the filters in your home frequently. Many toxins and pollutants are taken into the body through the lungs, and changing air filters is one way to help ensure that the air in your home or place of business is as pollutant-free as possible.

- *A good mattress and pillow.* Later, we'll discuss the importance of getting a good night's sleep. For many people, a bad mattress or pillow is the chief culprit that keeps a person from resting well. If your mattress is over ten years old, you probably need a new one. Pillows should be new every two or three years—they are great collectors of dust mites and other allergens.

- *Room-darkening shades or drapes.* Again, related to your sleep, research is showing that sleep occurs best in dark rooms. Consider investing in room-darkening shades or drapes if your bedroom is not sufficiently dark during your sleep times.

- *Exercise gear.* The two main keys when it comes to exercise gear are "fit" and "safety." Make sure that you have good walking, jogging, or running shoes that fit well, give adequate support to your feet, and are as comfortable as possible. Make sure your exercise clothing is loose and, if you are exercising outside, that you wear "layers" so you can maintain even body warmth. If you are planning to cycle or skate for exercise, make sure you have a good helmet and adequate elbow and knee pads. If you are swimming, consider earplugs and eye goggles, especially if you are swimming in a heavily chlorinated pool. If you are planning to exercise outside at night or before dawn, make sure you are wearing something reflective so you can be readily seen.

I personally do not recommend home gyms because the equipment available for the home market simply isn't as good as that in professional gyms, and because few people who purchase home workout systems rarely use them consistently or accurately. The exception is this: Two-pound or five-pound hand weights or ankle weights that you can carry with you as you walk or jog. You can actually make your own hand weights by filling small water bottles and carrying them with you—the water consumed at the end of your walk will help keep you hydrated! If walking or jogging is your preferred type of exercise, you may also want to purchase a pedometer—a small device that clips on to your waistband to measure the number of steps you take in a given exercise period of day. A good pedometer can be purchased for under twenty-five dollars.

## "He who doesn't climb the mountain cannot enjoy the view."

Finally, I recommend that you work with an exercise trainer or personal coach. One might be assigned to you at the gym where you work out. A trainer can help you with specific areas of body toning and also help you choose exercises, the amount of weights, and so forth, so you can receive maximum benefit from your exercise time without injury.

Ask at a reputable gym who might be available to work with you. Talk to several trainers before choosing one. Seek out a person with whom you feel comfortable and whom you trust to encourage you rather than nag you. Working with a good, qualified professional will help you from the outset of your plan to make sure that you do not develop any bad habits in your exercise routines.

COACH PAULA:

## Trade Up to *God's Best*

Jesus gave an interesting teaching to His followers. He said, "When the unclean spirit is gone out of a man, he walketh through dry places, seeking rest, and findeth none. Then he saith, I will return into my house from whence I came out; and when he is come, he findeth it empty, swept, and garnished. Then goeth he, and taketh with himself seven other spirits more wicked than himself, and they enter in and dwell there: and the last state of that man is worse than the first. Even so shall it be also unto this wicked generation" (Matthew 12:43–45).

It isn't enough for a person to turn from evil or bad. A person must embrace fully what is good and healthful—emotionally and spiritually as well as physically. We are responsible for creating, establishing, and renewing not only our physical bodies but also good relationships and good environments.

Let me be very direct and practical in this. Many people are living in bad to mediocre relationships and in bad to mediocre environments at the time they accept Jesus as their personal Savior. They experience a wonderful cleansing from sin, guilt, and shame in their inner spirit—but then they do nothing to cleanse their "outer" world. What generally needs to be changed?

Relationships that are unhealthy need to be exchanged for relationships that are healthy. I am not at all advocating simply walking out on an intimate relationship that is not functioning—in that case, I am telling you to get wise counsel and abide by it. If possible, turn the relationship into something good. Don't continue to live in a bad relationship where you are violated. If you are hanging out with people who are dragging you down emotionally and continually tempting you to go places or do things that you know are interfering with your walk and growth with God, end those relationships.

Don't stay in dead-end relationships with people who have no interest in going to heaven with you. Don't stay in abusive relationships in which you are a victim to the power plays of another person. Stand up on the inside...and walk away. God has something—and someone—better for you.

"But," you may be saying, "I need to stay in this relationship to win this person to Christ." If that is what the Lord is speaking to your heart, then you have an obligation to tell the person about Christ as soon as possible and with as much Christian compassion and love as possible. If the person accepts Christ, great! Take that person to church with you. Help that person get involved in Bible study and outreach services. But if the person does not accept Christ, move on. There is far more likelihood that a person who is resistant to Christ will draw you away from the Lord than you will draw that person to the Lord. There is a vast difference between "ministering" to a person and fellowshipping with them. Be honest with yourself when you evaluate your relationship and the impact they have on you.

At times, you may need to move—literally. You may need to move out of your apartment or house, out of your neighborhood, and perhaps even out of your city. Ask God what is best for you. Some environments simply are not GOOD emotionally or spiritually for you or your children. There is nothing to be gained by your staying in an environment that is filled with crime, immorality, and drugs.

*The best way not to revert to old unhealthful spiritual and emotional relationships and habits is to create NEW healthful ones.*

## *Find* a Good Church Home

One of the foremost challenges every person faces is finding a good church that preaches the Word of God fully and accurately, and where the presence of the Holy Spirit is welcome and His power is evident. Don't stay in a "dead" church. Find a place where you can express a living, vibrant faith. Find a place where you can learn the Word of God through good teaching and preaching. Find a place where you can discover the natural and spiritual gifts God has given to you, and where you can use them to serve others. Develop friendships with the people in that church.

## Take a Look at Your *Time, Activities, and Possessions*

Various aspects about the things you purchase and the way you spend your time may also need to be adjusted so that you are planting into your life what is GOOD for you spiritually and emotionally.

Rather than solely read the trashy novels and magazines you've been reading, start reading the Word of God. Read magazines and books that are inspirational and that build up your faith.

Likewise with what you watch. Rather than watching a television program or movie that feeds or produces "bad fruit" in your life, choose to go to or rent movies and programs that present good fruit. Get DVDs of good preaching and teaching that can help you grow in your faith.

Rather than hang out at the local bar or club, go to church.

Rather than spend your weekend partying, go on a retreat with friends, your spouse, your children, or a church group. Or get involved in a ministry that is making a difference in the lives of others.

Listen to music that enriches and nurtures your soul. If you can sing, get involved in the music ministry at your church or visit a nursing home and use your gift and talent to bless the often forgotten.

Every where you can, and in every way you can, trade in the old drag-you-down habits and patterns for God's new, creative, beautiful, productive habits and patterns.

Turn your mind to creative pursuits and especially to pursuits in which you can honor the Lord and serve others. I know a woman who discovered she had several more hours in a week after she quit hanging out at a nearby hotel lounge after work each day. She decided she was going to learn to bake. It was something she had always had an interest in doing. She took a couple of free cooking lessons and began trying various recipes. She developed her own bread baking ministry—making small loaves of whole-grain fruit bread and giving them to her neighbors with a little card, "I've discovered the Bread of Life. If you'd like to meet Him, give me a call." Jesus referred to Himself, of course, as the Bread of Life (John 6:35). This woman led more than a dozen people to the Lord, and soon after she became the founder and head of a ministry within her church that bakes loaves of bread and distributes them as a major evangelistic outreach into the poorest neighborhoods of that city. By the way, she made a number of new friends as part of this ministry, and one of the men who helped deliver the bread to the projects is now her fiancé!

Ask God to show you how and with what He desires for you to fill your days. Ask Him to send special people your way to be your mentors, teachers, coworkers, and friends.

The best way *not* to revert to old unhealthful spiritual and emotional relationships and habits is to create NEW healthful ones!

*Take active steps toward a new and healthier future.*
*It isn't enough merely to turn away from the bad*
*and toward the good—*
*you need to begin to walk down the*
*good road to greater wholeness!*

THE
# ten
## COMMANDMENTS
*of Health & Wellness*

# Commandment 4

## EAT THE RIGHT
## *Nutrients*
## IN MODERATION

*"Too much of a good thing is...
too much!"*

*COACH*
DODD:

## Six Meals a Day for *Better Health*

As suggested in an earlier chapter, I recommend that people eat six small meals a day. These meals need to be balanced, and they need to have enough variety so that over time a person doesn't become totally bored with food. Boredom, of course, is one of the main factors that can lead a person to seek out the wrong foods that give a sugar high. In the health plan at the back of this book, I refer to seven eating plans. Here they are:

### *Plan A*

#### Meal 1
One protein
One complex carb
One fibrous carb

#### Meal 2
Whey protein shake

#### Meal 3
One protein
One fibrous carb

#### Meal 4
Whey protein shake

#### Meal 5
One protein
One fibrous carb

## Meal 6

One whey protein shake

You'll find lists of protein and carb portions and items in the previous chapter. A complex carb—which is one serving of fruit or whole-grain cereal—can be substituted for any other complex carb.

## Plan B

There are no complex carbs on this day.

## Meal 1

One protein
One fibrous carb

## Meal 2

Whey protein shake

## Meal 3

One protein
One fibrous carb

## Meal 4

Whey protein shake

## Meal 5

One protein
One fibrous carb

## Meal 6

One whey protein shake

## Plan C

There are two complex carbs on this day—a serving of fruit or cereal can be substituted for any complex carb.

## Meal 1
One protein
One complex carb
One fibrous carb

## Meal 2
Whey protein shake

## Meal 3
One protein
One complex carb
One fibrous carb

## Meal 4
Whey protein shake

## Meal 5
One protein
One fibrous carb

## Meal 6
One whey protein shake

## *Plan L*

This day allows a "snack" item instead of a protein shake
and adds a bread item to the first two meals of the day.

## Meal 1
One protein
One complex carb
One fibrous carb
One bread or snack item

## Meal 2
Whey protein shake or snack

## Meal 3
One protein

One fibrous carb
One bread

## Meal 4

Whey protein shake or snack

## Meal 5

One protein
One fibrous carb

## Meal 6

One whey protein shake or snack

## Plan M

This day has three bread items. It is the day with the most food. Remember, one serving of fruit or cereal can be substituted for any complex carb.

## Meal 1

One protein
One complex carb
One fibrous carb
One bread

## Meal 2

Whey protein shake or snack

## Meal 3

One protein
One complex carb
One fibrous carb
One bread

## Meal 4

Whey protein shake

## Meal 5

One protein

One fibrous carb

One bread

## Meal 6

One whey protein shake or snack

## Plan N

This is a no complex-carb day, but nuts are added.

## Meal 1

One protein

One fibrous carb

One serving of cashews or almonds

## Meal 2

Whey protein shake

## Meal 3

One protein

One fibrous carb

1/2 avocado or one serving of nuts

## Meal 4

Whey protein shake

## Meal 5

One protein

One fibrous carb

One serving of cashews or almonds

## Meal 6

One whey protein shake

## Plan H

This is a high-carb day.

## Meal 1

One protein

Two complex carbs
One bread

## Meal 2

Whey protein shake or snack

## Meal 3

One protein
One complex carb
One fibrous carb
One bread

## Meal 4

Whey protein shake or snack

## Meal 5

One protein
One complex carb
One fibrous carb

## Meal 6

One whey protein shake or snack

Please note that every day's plan has a balance of protein and carbohydrates. This plan is neither a high-protein nor high-carb plan. It is a balanced approach to eating that can become a lifestyle. If a person does not have a balance in nutrients—or if one food group is excluded—that person will begin to crave what is missing, and cravings often lead to binge eating and a sequence of sugar highs and sugar lows that leave a person exhausted and discouraged.

Balanced nutrients in six small meals a day provides the maximum health benefit for sustained energy, strength, and a sense of well-being.

## Making These Plans *Work for YOU*

What I suggest you do is turn to the seven-week health plan at the back of the book and deal with only the first week you find there. You'll note that there is one day of eating according to PLAN L, three days of PLAN M, and one day of PLAN H. Plan out the foods you are going to eat on each of these days according to these plans. Personalize your food choices. In other words, pick foods you enjoy eating in each of these categories. Obviously, if you have any food allergies, such as an allergy to nuts, you will want to avoid those foods entirely.

*Balanced nutrients in six small meals a day provides the maximum health benefit for sustained energy, strength, and a sense of well-being.*

I've put "whey" protein on the plan because I believe this is the highest quality protein available in powder form, and it is the easiest protein source for some people to digest.

Below is a sample that one person constructed for herself for the first week's meals:

### Plan L

- 3 scrambled egg whites
- 1/2 cup oatmeal
- 1 cup blueberries
- 1 piece Ezekiel bread
- 1 whey shake
- 1 serving of diced tomatoes and cucumbers
- 1 piece Ezekiel bread
- 1 hummus and celery
- 1 chicken breast
- 1 serving steamed zucchini
- 1 serving sugar-free Jello
- 1 serving of canned tuna

## Plan M x 3

- 7 oz low-fat cottage cheese
- 1/2 cup oatmeal
- 1 peach
- 1 piece Ezekiel bread
- 1 whey shake
- 1 patty ground turkey grilled
- 1/2 yam
- 1 apple, diced and steamed
- 1 whey shake
- 1 portion white fish
- 1 lettuce salad with lemon
- 1 piece Ezekiel bread
- 1 serving sugar-free Jello

## Plan H

- 1 protein bar
- 1 plum
- 1 apple
- 1 piece Ezekiel bread
- 1 celery and almond butter
- 1 serving canned tuna
- 1 lettuce salad with veggies
- 1 piece Ezekiel bread
- nuts
- 1 beef steak
- 1 steamed artichoke/lemon
- 1/2 cup brown rice
- 1 serving sugar-free Jello

It will only take you a few minutes to refer to each plan and the food lists. After a while, you will probably have the food lists memorized, and the process will be even faster.

Then, after you have determined what YOU want to eat during the coming week, make your grocery list. Buy the foods you need. Pre-prepare any items that you want. And get ready to enjoy the week!

All of the food groups are covered in the various nutrition plans. The "mix" of those foods allows for tremendous choice and variety.

## *Portion Control* for *Moderation*

In the earlier chapter, I included portion sizes for various foods. Portion size varies, but only a little, according to your size. The portion size for a 220-pound man is going to be different than the portion size for a 120-pound woman...but only slightly. In most cases, the ounces and amounts identified in these plans are a guideline. A person once asked me, "Can I press down the lettuce and veggies to get a cup, or do I need to keep them fluffed up?" She was serious. The truth is, you can probably eat a head of lettuce and not gain an ounce of weight—you'll spend more calories chewing the lettuce than there are calories in the lettuce. I replied, "What feels like the right thing to you?" She nodded, and we left it at that. I have a hunch she presses down the lettuce and veggies to make one cup of complex carbs—and that's alright with me!

Over time, you'll discover the amount of food that you can take in and still maintain your optimal weight and energy level. The plan offered here is for seven weeks. Be disciplined in sticking to the program prescribed for at least that long. Then make variations according to your own body.

What I want to emphasize is that many times people take the phrase "all things in moderation" to mean that they can include unhealthful foods and practices into their lives, just as long as they don't "overdo" those practices. That isn't at all what it means to live, eat, and exercise in moderation! Moderation means to take in GOOD things in the amount your body needs, and nothing more.

Too much of a good thing...is still too much. At the same time...not enough of what's needed...is not enough. Moderation means finding what is right for your body in quantity, but moderation gives no license to eat lower-quality nutrients or to engage in harmful practices. Moderation is never a license to engage in any activity or eat foods that are bad for you in the long run of your life. For example, a man told me he had decided he was going to smoke cigars "in moderation"—for him, that meant three a week instead of one a day. That's not moderation. That's engaging in a lesser amount of something that isn't in any way healthful to his lungs and certainly not helpful to his wife's allergies!

Be wise in the choices you make. Seek variety in the foods you eat. Mix up your exercise plan. But stay within the guidelines of the plan for maximum results.

## COACH PAULA:

## The Word of God Is *Spiritual Food*

The Word of God refers to itself in terms of "food" for the spirit. Both the Book of Hebrews and 1 Corinthians refer to the Word of God in terms of "milk" and "meat." Hebrews tells us strong meat—in other words, the deep truths of God's Word—is essential for discerning fully "both good and evil" (Hebrews 5:14). The concept here is this: God's Word feeds our spirit at the level of our spiritual maturity. The Bible has something to say to every person, in every situation, of every age, and in every culture and nation…every day.

I have read the Bible through from cover to cover many times, and I can assure you of this—no human being will ever plummet all the depths of God's Word no matter how many times they read the Bible! There's always something new to learn, and there's always a new way to apply God's Word to your own life situations.

*Just as we need a balance in nutrients, we also need to take in the "whole" of God's Word.*

We all know the phrase, "You are what you eat." That's also true of God's Word. Those who take in the Word of God consistently and in increasing depth of study, "grow up" spiritually. They are healthy, continually renewed spiritual beings. There is no substitute for reading the Word of God. It is life to the spirit. It is what produces sharp discernment between good and evil. It is what prepares a person fully to walk in wisdom and make sound judgments and right choices hour by hour, day by day.

As human beings, we eat daily. We also need to be reading the Word of God daily.

Those who have done scientific and medical research into the body's chemistry tell us repeatedly the importance of eating breakfast each day. I heartily recommend that a person read the Word of God first thing in the morning. That's the best time to take in the truth of God's Word and see how God will apply that word to your life all day long.

Dodd recommends eating six small meals a day for even

energy flow. I certainly am all in favor of a person reading the Word of God multiple times during a day, even if it is only for five or ten minutes. Dodd taught you to prepare your food and make it convenient. I want you to do the same with your spiritual food. Beyond a dedicated time and place to read the Word each day, put a Bible in your bathroom, on the treadmill, and in the family room. In other words, incorporate the Word into your daily routines.

> "Winners find a way to make things work.
> Losers make excuses for why things don't work."

Just as we need a balance in nutrients, we also need to take in the "whole" of God's Word. I recommend that you read a portion of the Old Testament, a portion of the Psalms, a portion of the Book of Proverbs, a portion of the Gospels (Matthew, Mark, Luke, and John), and a portion of the other New Testament writings at least every week, if not a mix like this every day. As you do this over time, you will begin to make connections among various passages of the Bible, and you will stay balanced in your understanding of God's message to you.

Always read your Bible in this way:
- *Read a version of the Bible you understand easily.*
  There are a number of good translations and paraphrases on the market today.
- *Purchase and read a Bible that has good study notes in it.*
  I also recommend that you buy a Bible that has the

words of Jesus in red letters—that makes it easy to see clearly and at a glance what Jesus taught.

- *Before you begin reading, ask the Lord to help you understand what you read and to show you ways to apply His Word to your life.* After you finish reading, ask the Lord to seal that word into your life so you will never forget it and will begin to live according to it.

- *Memorize key verses that are especially related to your particular needs and circumstances.* Especially memorize verses that describe who you are in Christ Jesus and that encourage you to trust God in all things and at all times.

- *Periodically, dive deeper into God's Word to study what God has to say about a particular issue or subject, to study the whole of a book of the Bible or the whole of a person's life story.*

God has a message for you! Take time to discover it, and then live it out.

> *Whether eating or reading God's Word,*
> *be consistent! What we do EACH DAY*
> *creates both a foundation for*
> *greater wholeness and*
> *a lifetime of good habits.*

STAY CLEANSED • STAY
CLEANSED

STAY CLEANSED • STAY

# Commandment 5

## REMOVE TOXINS AND
## *Stay Cleansed*

*"Cleansing is an important aspect of
both physical and spiritual health."*

COACH
DODD:

## *Toxins* Are a *Major Enemy* of Health

A great number of diseases and chronic ailments are directly related to a buildup, over time, of toxins in the body. A toxin is anything that is harmful or poisonous to human tissue—beginning at the level of each cell in the body. Toxins can be chemical, viral, bacterial, fungal, or parasites.

One of the main places that toxins build up is in the digestive tract, and especially the colon. Most people do not realize that a vast number of diseases are the result of poor digestive and colon health. Fatty deposits build up especially in the large intestine and colon, and this keeps good nutrients from moving into the bloodstream and also keeps waste products from being eliminated from the body regularly. The longer food "rots" in the intestines and colon, the greater the toxicity level of the material that does pass into the bloodstream.

For this reason, among others, I recommend that a person begin my health plan with a 24-Hour Cleanse.

## A 24-Hour *Cleanse*

For the first 24 hours of the health plan, a person eats no solid food. Instead, the person drinks six to twelve ten-ounce glasses of "Master Cleanse" lemonade drink. This is an all natural drink that has a very simple recipe you make yourself:

- One squeezed lemon
- Cayenne pepper to taste (about 1/10th of a teaspoon)
- One teaspoon Grade B maple syrup. This syrup must be organic. It can be purchased at a natural food or nutrition store.

These items are mixed with

- 10 ounces of fresh, pure spring water.

The lemonade drink can be consumed cold or hot. Make each glass fresh—in all, you'll need 6–12 lemons and 6–12 teaspoons of Grade B maple syrup.

At the end of the day, drink *one cup of herbal laxative tea.*

Starting the health plan this way does two things: First, it does a great deal to cleanse the digestive tract physically. Second, it does something to the "attitude" or thinking of the person who is starting a plan. It sends a message, "I, with God's help, am in control of what I eat and do; food is not in control of me."

Fasting is always empowering in ways that are not only physical. A fast is a signal to a person that he or she is *capable* of gaining control of out-of-control health habits and of exercising the discipline necessary to develop new habits.

## Staying Adequately Hydrated Is a Must

Most of your body is made of water. Sufficient water is necessary for the health of every cell in the body, every tissue, and every physical organ and system. Water is critical to blood flow and good digestion. And the truth is, most people do not drink enough water.

How much water do you need?

Weigh yourself. Divide your weight by 2. That's how many *ounces* of water you should drink daily.

| | |
|---|---|
| *Pounds of weight:* _____ *divided by 2 =* _____ *ounces* | |

To get the number of cups, divide the number of ounces by 8. For example, a 176-pound person needs 88 ounces of water a day, which is 11 cups. Most women, according to medical research, need 7 to 9 cups of water a day. Most men need 9 to 12 cups of water a day.

Water is certainly a part of other drinks and also fruits and vegetables, but for the seven weeks of the health plan, I encourage you to stick to pure water in sufficient quantity. You likely will be losing a significant amount of weight on this plan, and also flushing out toxins that may have been in your body for some time, and you will need adequate water to flush these fat globules and toxins from your system.

Also be aware that some beverages are *counterproductive* to water intake. For example, for every cup or glass of caffeinated beverage you consume, you should drink *two* cups or glasses of pure water. Actually, when it comes to coffee, I recommend that a coffee drinker consider switching to green tea and give their body a break from the tannic acid in coffee. Plus, green tea has thermogenic and fat oxidation properties—it has been proven to prevent the absorption of fat and to help the body burn fat faster. Chemicals in green tea have also been shown to shut down a key molecule that can play a significant role in the development of cancer.

Drink water throughout the day. Have a glass of water twenty to thirty minutes before you eat a small meal. You'll feel more satisfied by the food you eat and have less desire to overeat, plus this is a great "schedule" for taking in water throughout the day. Especially have a glass of water before you exercise, and again after you complete an exercise session.

> "Visualize how you want to look and imagine how you want to feel...and don't stop until you fulfill your vision and feel great!"

When eating out, make water—perhaps with a wedge of lemon or lime—your beverage of choice.

"Won't all this water make me feel bloated?" you may ask.

The exact opposite is true. When a person doesn't take in enough water, a signal is sent out from the brain, "We need to hoard water. We aren't getting enough." Water is retained, and the person feels bloated. On the other hand, when a person does take in enough water, the signal is sent, "We're getting all the water we need. We don't need to hoard water. We can use water to flush out the cells and tissues of fat and toxins."

"Won't I be going to the bathroom a lot?" you may ask.

Perhaps. This will even out over time. But going to the bathroom is not a bad thing when it comes to ridding your body of toxic wastes. That's exactly what you *want* to do!

You want to get rid of all the excess fat, unhealthful bacteria, and waste poisons you can—as quickly as you can.

Water is not only essential for full digestion of foods, but also for regular elimination of waste products. If you are traveling, and especially if you are taking long flights or find yourself sedentary for long periods, make sure you drink sufficient water to maintain regular elimination.

I realize that bodily elimination is not a subject most people are comfortable talking or reading about, but it is critical that you know a couple of things. First, good health is directly linked to a person having from one to three bowel movements a day, without any bloody discharge and without excessive strain. Colon cancer—in fact, all forms of cancer not related to smoking or a strong genetic history—is very rare in people who have at least one bowel movement a day. Most people in the United States are not this "regular." Antacids, digestive aids, and laxatives are among the top selling products in America's drugstores. Simple, calorie-free fiber would be of far more advantage to most people than these chemical products. If you need a laxative, use a natural herbal tea.

For many people, and especially those over the age of forty, natural "digestive enzymes" are very helpful. I usually recommend a chewable papaya enzyme product. These enzymes help break down food so that it is more readily digested *fully*, which results in less "gas" in the digestive tract.

## Eat Sufficient Fibrous Foods

The second major thing you can do in cleansing your digestive tract is to eat enough fiber. That's one of the reasons this health plan breaks down nutrients into a category called "fibrous carbohydrates." Why fiber? Several reasons: First, fiber adds to a feeling of being full and satisfied. Second, fiber gently "scrubs" the walls of the intestine and colon to cleanse fat and toxins from the walls of these organs—which, in turn, allows for more nutrients to be absorbed by the body. Third, fiber absorbs toxins and fat and allows these "poisons" to be eliminated with minimal damage to the body.

Vegetables and fruit are good "fiber" foods. Be sure to leave the "skin" on whenever possible. Raw vegetables and fruit have maximum fiber content. The pectin in an apple is an extremely good source of fiber.

Whole grains are also rich in fiber. The "husk" of the grain must be present for grain to have fiber value. Grains that have been processed to eliminate the husk, such as the flour for white bread, break down in the body into a mass of "goo" that has something of the consistency of glue. This goo is slow to pass through the system and actually inhibits the absorption of good nutrients into the bloodstream.

If you aren't getting enough fiber into your system, you may need to supplement your fiber intake with capsules or beverages designed for this purpose. Make sure the fiber sources you may add to your health plan do not have sugar hidden among the ingredients.

## Consistency Is Key

It isn't enough to drink enough water one day and ignore water the next. The same for fiber. Consistency is key.

Periodically—in fact, about every seven weeks—you may want to fast a day. Give your body a break from the work of digestion. Repeat the 24-Hour Cleanse recommended at the beginning of this chapter.

*COACH*
PAULA:

## The Role of *Fasting* in a Person's *Spiritual Life*

There are two spiritual principles that parallel what Dodd has shared in this chapter. The first is the principle of fasting—which means going without all food in a day or without particular types of food over a period of time. Of course, you continue to drink plenty of water and stay well hydrated. Fasting is linked in God's Word with prayer. The purpose of fasting is to turn a person's heart away from the physical and material life and toward the inner spiritual life. It is to put the focus on spiritual things, with the understanding that life *at its core* is spiritual. It is the spirit of man that has the capacity for everlasting life. It is the spirit of man that births all true creativity and innovation. It is the spirit of man that is the source of love, which is the foundation for all good relationships.

Prayer, coupled with fasting, is powerful in ways that cannot be adequately described. They must be experienced in order to be fully appreciated. Prayer opens a person up to God—deepening and strengthening a person's relationship with God. Fasting "shuts down" a person's natural intake from the physical world in order to allow for an increased spiritual intake directly from God.

I know some people who fast one meal a week to spend time in intense prayer; others who undertake a three-day fast once a month, and still others who begin each year with a time of limited fasting and prayer that spans several weeks. Ask God what He desires for you. (I recommend you get my book *Fasting Made Simple*.)

> *Seeking forgiveness and giving forgiveness are ongoing processes. Every hurt, grudge, or grievance you hold in your heart becomes toxic to your spirit.*

## The Role of *Cleansing*

There simply is no substitute for spiritual cleansing—in simple terms, cleansing in the Word of God is linked directly to *forgiveness*. The prophet Isaiah gave these words from God: "Come now, and let us reason together," says the LORD, "though your sins are like scarlet, they shall be as white as snow; though they are red like crimson, they shall be as wool" (Isaiah 1:18). When King David prayed for forgiveness, he prayed: "Purge me with hyssop, and I shall be clean; wash me, and I shall be whiter than snow.... Create in me a clean heart, O God, and renew a steadfast spirit within me" (Psalm 51:7, 10).

If you have never asked God to forgive you of your sins

and to give you a clean, new heart, today is the day! God longs to forgive you so He can be fully restored in right relationship to you. Sin is like toxins in your spirit—sin poisons a person's outlook, keeps a person from taking in God's blessings, and blocks a person's ability to know God. The word *sin* in its original context means "to miss the mark." The Bible teaches us that we all have missed the mark, but God who loves us unconditionally sent His Son to put us back "on track." Forgiveness is the only acceptable antidote for sin, guilt, and shame. I encourage you to pray this prayer aloud with a sincere heart:

> *"God, I believe that Jesus is Your Son whom You sent to die as a sacrifice for the sins of the world, including my sin. I accept what Jesus did as being on my behalf. I ask You to forgive me and to cleanse me of all my sin. I ask You to create a new desire within me to love You and obey You and to help me turn away from everything that would keep me from developing a deep relationship with You. I believe that You are forgiving me right now, according to the promises in Your Word. Amen."*

Just as in the physical realm we need ongoing cleansing, so too spiritual cleansing is an ongoing process. Seeking forgiveness and giving forgiveness are ongoing processes. Every hurt, grudge, or grievance you hold in your heart becomes toxic to your spirit.

End every day asking God to forgive you for those things that you have done that were not in full obedience to

His commandments. Then receive that forgiveness, knowing that the moment you asked, it was done. You'll sleep better and be better prepared for the tasks and challenges of the next day!

## Seeking *Forgiveness* From Other People

In addition to asking God for forgiveness, the Lord calls us to live in right relationship with other people. The apostle Paul wrote, "If it is possible, as much as depends on you, live peaceably with all men" (Romans 12:18). The only way to live in genuine peace with other people is to forgive others quickly and to ask for forgiveness without pride or hesitation when you have hurt another person. Jesus taught, "Forgive, and you will be forgiven" (Luke 6:37). In fact, Jesus said, "If you forgive men their trespasses, your heavenly Father will also forgive you. But if you do not forgive men their trespasses, neither will your Father forgive your trespasses" (Matthew 6:14–15). Forgiveness is not a "nice idea" in God's Word—it is a commandment, it is a requirement.

When a person lives in a state of forgiveness before God and in relationship with other people, there's no end to how God can bless that person. All of the gifts and blessings of God can flow freely into that person's life. All that is not of God is quickly eliminated—it does not fester and brew into anger, rage, bitterness, hatred, and other emotions that eventually can kill a person's soul and relationships.

I found that forgiveness is a choice. Perhaps you feel as though you have been violated too much to forgive that person. I understand and have been there. However, forgiveness is not only for the other person but its greatest benefit is for you. Nothing is worth bringing "cancer" to your soul. It dawned on me one day after going through the "confession of forgiveness" but never having the release of it that if God could put love in our hearts (Romans 5:5), He could place forgiveness there as well. I asked the Holy Spirit through this simple prayer to release me from any unforgiveness. This was my prayer: "God, I surrender to you the ability to put forgiveness in my heart where there has been offense, hurt, and wounding." Immediately, the Holy Spirit did a marvelous work within me that caused a transformation and release from the wounding that had occurred. God will do the same for you...simply ask.

Choose today to forgive and to seek forgiveness. Stay cleansed!

*Ask God to cleanse you today...*
*from the inside out,*
*and in every area of your being.*

### THE

# ten

## COMMANDMENTS

*of Health & Wellness*

# *Commandment 6*

## MOVE
# *More*

*"Exercise and ministry both involve
expenditures of energy and effort."*

COACH
DODD:

## Different *Exercises* for Different *Benefits*

Exercise is any activity, movement, or task aimed at keeping a person strong and healthy. Given that basic definition of exercise, a person can exercise his or her body, his mind, his spirit, his talents, his skills, and any other aspect of his being. Physical exercise involves physical exertion—it is a "putting out" of effort and an expenditure of energy. The return is a little ironic—exercise results in greater ease of effort and motion and a renewal of energy. Rather than make a person tired, exercise invigorates. Rather than weaken a person's resources or reduce a person's reserves, exercise makes a person stronger. Rather than add stress, exercise alleviates stress. Exercise reduces appetite and improves sleep.

*There are very few things that cost less and do more for a person's health and wholeness than regular physical exercise.*

Regular physical exercise has been shown to improve a person's sense of total well-being—it has benefits to the emotions, soul, mind, and spirit. Most people who exercise routinely believe that exercise helps them think clearer, feel less tension and anxiety, and enjoy life more.

Even moderate physical activity daily can reduce substantially a person's risk of developing or dying from cardiovascular disease, Type II diabetes, and certain cancers, such as colon cancer. Daily physical activity helps lower blood pressure and both LDL (bad) cholesterol and total cholesterol. It helps prevent osteoporosis, obesity, anxiety, depression, and arthritis. Plus, a thirty-minute or longer walk can increase calorie burning in the body for seven to ten hours after the walk is completed. This can help tremendously in weight loss.

There are very few things that cost less and do more for a person's health and wholeness.

There are three different types of physical exercise that I recommend to my clients. As in the case of nutrients, different types of exercises produce different benefits, and all three forms of exercise are included in the seven-week health plan. A variety of exercises also helps keep a person from getting bored and keeps a person more motivated to continue an exercise program. Specifically, I recommend that a person have:

- a basic total body conditioning workout.
- a commitment to "walking for life."
- a foundational stretching routine.

Let me address the first two of these in a little more detail in this chapter. I'll deal with stretching in the next chapter.

## A Basic *Total Body* Conditioning *Workout*

My total body conditioning workout is based upon a set of eleven exercises. On the following pages are explanations for each exercise and a summary of how they go together.

## 1 | Jogging in Place

Standing on a cushioned surface, bring your knees up as high as possible as you jog in place. Strive for a "soft landing," trying to prevent any excessive pounding or any jarring movements. In the beginning, try to complete one full minute, and as the weeks go by, add another 20 to 30 seconds each week. The goal is to be jogging in place three to five minutes by the seventh week.

## Chair Squats | 2

Place a sturdy chair behind you. Spread your feet shoulder-width apart. Place your arms horizontally in front of you. Then s-l-o-w-l-y squat down until your posterior touches the chair…but only briefly. Do not sit down! Come back up to the starting position. Keep your head up and your back straight as you do this. Do not lock your knees when you are standing. In my experience as a trainer, I have found that doing chair squats in a slow controlled manner builds the most muscle fiber in a person's legs.

## 3 | Counter Push-Ups

Put both hands on a kitchen counter approximately shoulder-width apart. Straighten your arms as if you were going to do a push-up. Then take a couple of steps back, keeping your feet in line and close together. Bend your arms and slowly lower your body until your chest touches the counter. Immediately reverse direction and push back up into the starting position. This movement should be performed in a smooth controlled motion while keeping the muscles under tension.

In a standing position with your feet shoulder-width apart, raise your hands a little wider than shoulder-width apart toward the sky or ceiling. Keep your legs straight and your hips back. Slowly bend forward while twisting your torso and reach down and place your right hand on your left foot. Return to your starting position. Reach down again and place your left hand on your right foot. If you can't reach all the way to your foot, reach down as far as you can comfortably without bending your legs and without undo pain in the back of your leg. Do not do this exercise too fast, as it could cause lightheadedness. Make this a slow and controlled stretching exercise.

## 5 | Squat Dips

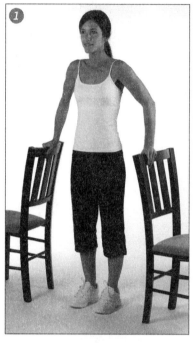

Place two tables or heavy chairs that are the same height about 24–36 inches apart. Stand with your feet slightly apart and centered between the tables or chairs and place one hand on each of the chairs or tables at your side. Then squat straight down, allowing the pressure to stay on your triceps, which are the muscles at the back of the upper arm. Your legs will be working, but your main purpose in this exercise is a workout of your upper arms. Do this exercise slow and steady, keeping pressure on your triceps at all times.

## Standing Calf Raises | 6

In a standing position, raise your body up on "tip toes" as high as possible. Hold this position of standing on the balls of your feet for two seconds before coming back down.

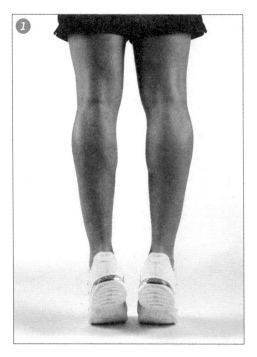

## 7 | *One-Legged Accordions*

While lying flat on your back on the floor with your arms straight out directly over your head against the floor, pretend your left leg is a drawbridge being raised up. Raise your leg as far as possible, with only a slight bend at the knee. At the same time, bring your arms forward, while curling your torso forward at the same time. Touch your left knee with both hands at the same time. Hold this for a count of two while contracting your abdominal muscles, then drop back down into the starting position. Repeat by raising your right leg as far as possible and touching your right knee with both hands as you curl your body and legs forward.

## Two-Legged Accordions | 8

While lying on the floor, flat on your back with your arms stretched out flat over your head, pretend BOTH legs are a drawbridge. Raise them up together with only a slight bend. (Your legs should be almost straight.) At the same time, curl your torso toward your knees, bringing your arms forward. Touch your knees, one hand on each knee. Hold for a count of two, then slowly extend back down into the starting position.

## 9 | Leg Lifts

While lying flat on the floor, place both hands under the small of your back for support. Bring your knees up toward your chest as far as possible. Hold for a count of one while contracting your abdominal muscles, then slowly extend your legs back to the starting position.

## Chair Crunches | 10

Place a chair in front of you. Sit down on the floor and lie back until your head is resting on the floor. Now raise both feet and calves and place them on the chair. With your hands out in front of you, angled up toward the chair, curl your torso forward until you can't go any farther. Hold this for a count of two, then slowly extend back to the starting position.

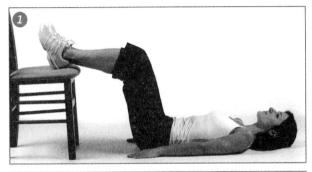

## 11 | Booty Busters

Get down on all fours and kick your right leg, like a donkey, toward the sky. Hold this position for a count of two while squeezing your right gluteus (butt) muscle, and then return to the starting position. Kick out with your left leg, like a donkey—your ankle should be as high toward the sky or ceiling as it can go. Again, hold for a count of two as you squeeze your left gluteus (butt) muscle. Return to the starting position. If this exercise begins to feel too "easy" for you, buy ankle weights for added resistance. Start with five-pound weights. Eventually, you may be able to handle ten-pound ankle weights.

Perspiration is a way of ridding the body of toxins. Don't be afraid to perspire when you exercise. It's a sign of health.

*Putting It All Together.* I suggest that you turn on some good inspirational music—whatever gets your blood going. Okay, get ready and here we go...

Jog for one minute in place. (Eventually, you'll be jogging in place for three to five minutes.) Keep your knees up as high as possible. Try to make soft steps with your feet. No pounding. Think light on your feet.

As soon as you catch your breath, which should take no more than thirty seconds, do your chair squats. Then do the counter push-ups. After your push-ups, move into windmills. Do squat dips and calf raises. Support yourself with a chair or countertop if necessary.

Then lie on the floor and do the one-legged accordion, two-legged accordion, and leg lifts.

Get up and do your chair crunches. Roll over on to all fours and do your booty busters.

Congratulations! You just did more work than most people do spending half the day in a gym!

## Walking for Life

I believe there are two basic categories of people: People who are living and seeking more out of life, and people who are slowly dying. Those who are dying have stopped moving and trying to improve their lives. The ones who are seeking more out of life are moving and fighting! I want you to be a person who is living and always seeking more out of life.

The simplest and most productive exercise motion that human beings can make is *walking*. We were created to walk upright. To be able to stand and walk is a sure sign a person is alive. (How many times did Jesus say, "Take up your bed...and *walk*." I believe He was saying, "Take up your life...and walk!")

## "Focus on progress, not perfection, in order to build confidence."

As stated earlier, make sure you have a quality pair of walking shoes and that you wear cushioned socks. Grab a bottle of pure water to take with you so you can stay hydrated, and then lace on your shoes and head out on a walk!

I encourage you to take a look at the overall health plan at the back of the book. You'll find for the first day 7/7 = 14. That simply means to walk seven minutes in one direction, then turn around and go back. Try to maintain your same pace of walking in both directions. You'll be walking a total of fourteen minutes.

How fast should you walk? I believe the best pace is the one you would use if you were late for an airline flight and were trying to get to the gate as fast as possible without running.

If walking alone seems easy for you, try to alternate walking and jogging, a few minutes of each. Whatever it takes to make it more challenging! You certainly can jog the entire time if your conditioning is strong.

Whenever possible, walk outside. Fifteen to twenty minutes of sunshine each day is great for the body and helps the body produce vitamin D. On days of intense sunshine, take a hat to put on after twenty minutes. Too much sun can cause skin cancer.

Over the seven weeks of the plan, you'll be walking more. Try to maintain a quick pace even as you add a few minutes to your walk every few days.

COACH PAULA:

## A *Focused Expenditure* of Spiritual Energy and Effort

I believe the spiritual counterpart to physical exercise is *ministry.*

Physical exercise involves a person doing more than a person would normally do. Every person is active and in motion to some extent. Exercise is being *more* active and engaging in *more* movement and doing so in a way that is intentional, focused, repetitive, and regular. In a very similar manner, every person is involved with other people to some extent. No person is self-contained or totally isolated from humanity. Every person has opportunities every day to engage in random acts of kindness. Ministry is a matter of being *more* actively involved with other people in ways that are highly intentional, focused, and consistent. Ministry involves an expenditure of spiritual energy and effort. Ministry involves a continual and regular rendering of loving service.

By ministry I am not at all referring to a full-time church-related job. I am referring to the giving of a person's talents, time, and spiritual gifts to other people who are in need.

Sharing the good news of Jesus with those who have never heard it…

Feeding the hungry…

Giving shelter to the homeless…

Mentoring and tutoring young children in basic reading and writing skills…

Singing in the choir or at the nursing home…

Teaching a Sunday school class or working in a vacation church school program…

Cleaning and repairing church facilities or a widow's home…

Distributing school supplies and clothes to needy children…

The giving of money to help build an orphanage or hospital as part of a missionary outreach…

Taking flowers to those who are homebound…

Delivering a meal to a grieving family…

Visiting those who are in prisons and hospitals…

Saying a kind word with a warm smile and gentle hug.

All of these are acts of loving service, and when they are done in the Name of Christ Jesus, they are "ministry." The opportunities for ministry are endless because human needs are endless. The expressions that ministry might take are unlimited. Ask the Lord to reveal to you what specifically He has for you to do, and then ask when, where, how, and with whom you might fulfill His call on your life. Ministry very often involves working with others as a team. Look for the "team" that has an opening for your specific talents and abilities.

Every act of genuine Christ-honoring ministry has these qualities:

- the act of loving service is intended to benefit the person who receives the service far more than to call attention to the giver of the service.
- the act of loving service brings glory to Christ Jesus.
- the act of loving service is performed in a faithful, genuine, honest, and joyful manner that is consistent with the way Jesus treated those who were sick, spiritually oppressed, or in any kind of need.
- the act of loving service is performed as a commitment between the giver and God—the service is rendered "as unto the Lord," as if the person receiving the service might be Christ Jesus Himself.

Just as in the case of exercise, ministry doesn't just "happen." Good ministry takes planning, a degree of organization and administration, and a commitment to *regular* service. Ministry is marked by *faithfulness and steadfastness.* A person who is present one day to help and absent the next is *not* a faithful minister. The ministry that such a person renders is going to be far less effective than ministry that can be "counted on" by others who may be involved on the same ministry team or be among those who receive ministry care.

People tend to know me today because they see me on television or preaching before large audiences. That is not where my ministry began! I started in "ministry" by volunteering to clean the little church I was attending. I did it with as much excellence as I could. The pastor eventually entrusted me to work in the nursery holding and diapering babies during the church service. Then he asked me to teach the toddlers. It wasn't until after I had worked in a number of very practical ministries for many years, including major outreaches of food and material goods to the poorest neighborhoods of my city, that I was actually invited to speak on a platform before a group of people! Be faithful in the ministry where God places you. Ask those in authority at your church to help you plug in to ministries so you can meet practical needs. Find the need and fulfill the call. Serve with excellence and faithfulness. No ministry is too small in God's eyes. He grows great trees from small seeds!

The goal of all ministry is not to keep people in need of ministry, but rather to help people to the point that those who once received ministry *become* ministers. Ministry involves equipping people to trust God in new ways, to help people develop their God-given talents and gifts to greater levels, and to motivate others to become "givers" who will extend and enlarge a particular area of ministry.

God calls every person to some form of ministry. That's the reason you have the talents and abilities you have—so you might develop them and then give them away in service to other people!

Does ministry take time? Yes.

Does it take ongoing effort? Yes.

Does it mean that on occasion a person may be near the exhaustion point from having given so much? Absolutely.

But the benefits of ministry are also similar to the benefits of regular exercise. The faithful minister is not depleted by what he gives to others—he is refreshed, renewed, and rejuvenated. The faithful minister does not have fewer skills or abilities as a result of his loving service—his skills and abilities are enhanced, enlarged, developed, and made stronger. The faithful minister does not have a feeling of "less" but rather feelings of "more" satisfaction, fulfillment, and joy.

> *God calls every person to some form of ministry. That's the reason you have the talents and abilities you have—so you might develop them and then give them away in service to other people.*

Physical exercise produces both temporary and long-range benefits.

The spiritual exercise of ministry produces earthly satisfaction and everlasting rewards.

Physical exercise should be a regular part of what you do for your body, for the rest of your life. Finding and then being faithful in the pursuit of your ministry should be the very core of what you "do" for the Lord, for all eternity.

*It's the EXTRA effort that produces
the greatest benefits—both in physical
exercise and in spiritual ministry.*

BREATH AND STRETCH •

BREATH AND STRETCH •

BREATH AND STRETCH •

# Commandment 7

## LET GO OF
## *Excess Stress*

*"Stress is a problem
that can be solved!"*

## *Stress* Can Be Reduced Greatly!

If there's one word that seems to define the way many people feel about their lives today, it is the word *stressful.* We live in a society that attempts to pack way too much into too little time. We are people, it seems, who have taken on more responsibilities than can fit in most days. Many people have become so accustomed to stress, they don't even seem to know how stressed they are. And they don't seem to realize how dangerous stress can be.

Certainly, a degree of stress is inevitable. We do not exert ourselves in any way—from doing simple chores to perspiration-generating work tasks—without creating some level of stress for our bodies. A small amount of stress from time to time is important for us to flee from dangerous situations or take action to better a situation. It is *excess* stress that we must address. Stress that is too intense for too long a period is *excess* stress. This includes moderate levels of stress that are allowed to continue for long periods of time. The end result is a depletion of the adrenal-cortisol system of the body. When that happens, the immune system is impaired, and a person can readily become host to a wide variety of degenerative diseases. Excess stress also disrupts the digestive process and can interfere with sleep.

Excess stress is manifested in the body by two main outward and visible signs:

- stiff, tense muscles
- shallow breathing

Monitor your own muscles tension right now. Clench your hand into a fist and hold that clenched position for a few seconds, then release your hand to a relaxed position. The tension and tightness you felt in your hand muscles may very well be the state of other muscles in your body at a slightly lower level of tension—but tension nonetheless. How tense are the muscles of your neck? How much tension do you feel in the muscles across your upper back and shoulders?

*Although moments of stress from time to time may be motivating and stimulating, prolonged periods of lower levels of stress are dangerous and can be deadly.*

Tension in muscles eventually produces stiffness. It is my personal belief that a stiff body is an old body. The key to rejuvenating tense, stiff muscles is stretching.

Monitor your own breathing. Are you breathing in a shallow way? Is your breathing rapid? Do you feel at times as if you need more air? Constricted breathing leads to lower oxygen levels in the brain and body, and, over time, this constriction impacts all the internal organs of the body, also making them a little more tense and stiff. We often talk about the danger of hardened arteries—the truth is, no organ of the body should be "hard." A healthy body is flexible, from the inside out.

## *Stretching* to Reduce Stress

Watch a baby or toddler as he awakens from a nap or in the morning. The first thing that child does is likely to be "s-t-r-e-t-c-h." The same is true for most animals as they awaken from sleep. They stretch! We adult human beings are the only creatures who seem to think we have to hit the floor running. Take time to stretch when you awaken. If you have been sitting for a while, stand and stretch. Stop periodically in every day to stretch. Stretching helps blood flow as well as releases tension.

In my seven-week health plan, I also call for you to spend time every few days stretching. This stretching routine has eight specific stretching exercises. Taken together, they stretch all the major muscles in the body.

"The world always looks brighter from behind a smile."

As you stretch, always stretch slowly and carefully. Listen to your body and do not stretch beyond the point of pain. Move slowly through each of the stretching exercises. Never bounce or jerk your muscles. F-e-e-l each stretch. Feel your muscles elongating and then relaxing and loosening as you do each movement. Gradually increase your range of motion with each repetition of a stretching exercise.

Hold each stretch for thirty to forty-five seconds. Count out these seconds slowly.

Stretch until you feel a muscle tighten…but never stretch until you feel pain.

Stretch slowly, and again, don't "bounce."

## Hamstring Stretch | 1

Sit on the floor with your legs stretched out in front of you, your feet together. The goal is to touch your toes while keeping your knees flat against the floor. Do this two times with a thirty-second hold once you touch your toes.

## 2 | Straddle Stretch

Sit on the floor with your legs spread as far apart as possible. Then reach down your right hand and grab the right side of your upper right foot while keeping your leg completely straight—bend your torso over and try to kiss your knee. Repeat for the left side. Reach out with your left hand and grab the left side of your upper left feet, trying to kiss your left knee. Hold each stretch for forty-five seconds on each side.

## The Pancake | 3

Sit on the floor with your legs spread in a V position. Drop your torso down in the center of your legs and try to flatten your torso out like a pancake on the floor. Do this two times, holding the stretch for forty-five seconds each time.

## 4 | Knee Bend/Leg Extension

Lie on our back and pull your right leg slowly toward your chest, while keeping your left leg straight and flexing your toes so they are in a pointed position. Then do this for your right leg. Hold each leg at your chest for thirty seconds.

## Seal Stretch | 5

Flip over on to all fours. Drop your hips toward the floor, arching your lower back inward, keeping your chest up and with your eyes looking toward heaven. Hold the stretch for thirty seconds.

## 6 | Mad Dog Stretch

On all fours, take a mad dog stance—your glutes (butt muscles) should be raised up, arching your lower back as if you were making a saddle while keeping your chest up and arching. Hold the position for thirty seconds.

## Mad Cat Stretch | 7

On all fours, arch your back up as if someone hooked a cable to your upper back and is pulling you toward the sky. Hold the arched position for thirty seconds.

## 8 | Standing Quad Stretch

Brace yourself with your right arm against a counter, table, or sturdy chair, and then with your left arm, reach back and grab your left leg with your left hand. Pull your foot upward until it reaches your glutes (butt muscles). Hold your foot in that position for thirty seconds. Then repeat for the right arm and right leg.

Stretching is different than the total body conditioning exercises in that it requires patience and calmness. This perhaps is why stretching also works in a spiritual way to help a person "relax." Regard stretching as a form of "quiet time." I recommended previously that you turn on upbeat, motivating music for your total body conditioning workout. I recommend now that when you *stretch*, you listen to soothing, relaxing music or perhaps nature sounds (such as the surf at a beach or the sound of gently falling rain).

## *Breathing* to Reduce Stress

As amazing as it may seem, scientists tell us that seventy-five percent of all the toxins we take into our bodies are taken in through our lungs. Research in recent years has also linked the length and quality of a person's life to lung capacity—the greater a person's lung function and lung capacity, the greater the person's health tends to be.

Individually, we all know that at times we feel a need to stop and take a deep breath—the pause for deeper breathing is a moment for relieving stress and slowing the pace of our lives. On a more consistent basis, just as with exercise, regular times of deep breathing can result in great stress relief.

Therapeutic deep breathing is done using the diaphragm, the muscle just below the rib cage. Few people can feel this muscle directly—it seems to most people to be a "stomach area" muscle. To get a feel for deep breathing, lie on your back and place one hand on your stomach just below your rib cage and one hand on your upper chest.

Inhale. As you inhale, try to make your stomach rise—as opposed to your chest—and as you exhale, push with your stomach-area muscles to make your stomach "fall" as flat as possible. Then inhale again, relaxing your stomach muscles so the air seems to cause your stomach to rise. Push the air out of your lungs with your stomach muscles. If you do this type of breathing while standing up, your shoulders should not rise and fall as you breathe—rather, your abdominal muscles should appear to be moving in and out slightly.

*Just a few minutes a day in deep breathing and slow stretching can have amazing results in reducing a person's stress level.*

You don't need very many deep breaths to create a relaxing, stress-reducing result. Six to twelve breaths is sufficient. I recommend that you close your eyes as you breathe this way. See yourself in your mind's eye inhaling God's goodness and blessing and exhaling anything negative or problem-causing in your life. See yourself inhaling relaxation and exhaling stress.

Spend several minutes deep breathing and resting with your eyes closed—you'll likely be amazed at how just a few minutes of this can renew your energy and help you refocus on what is important to do next in your day. You may want to practice deep breathing several times in a day.

There are many variations on deep breathing exercises. You might try breathing in through your nostrils and exhaling through your mouth. You might try breathing in very slowly, expanding your lungs as much as possible. You might try exhaling slowly, pushing all the air you can out of your lungs. All of these are exercises that strengthen the lungs, bring more fresh air into your lungs, and aid in stress-reducing relaxation.

Most of all, it is important that you breathe in clean fresh air. Be very disciplined in changing the air filters of your home periodically. Avoid pollution-intense environments, including smoke-filled rooms. By all means, find a way to quit smoking if you are a smoker. A significant number of smokers say that they began smoking in order to experience a nicotine-induced sense of calm. In the long run, however, smoking causes far more internal stress on a person's body than nicotine ever produced in terms of a calming effect!

One added word—if you have sleep apnea, often indicated by snoring that is irregular—make sure that you address this problem. Sleep apnea is a serious breathing disorder that can have damaging health effects. Talk to your physician.

COACH PAULA:

## God's Answer for *Anxiety*

One of the most dramatic scenes in the New Testament resulted in Jesus raising a man named Lazarus from death. Even as Jesus called Lazarus back to life, and as Lazarus came walking out of the tomb in which he had been buried, Jesus said six power-filled words to those who witnessed Lazarus' return to life: "Loose him, and let him go."

What a message that is to people today in our fast-paced, over-obligated, stressed-out world!

Lazarus had been buried as all people were buried in that time. Long strips of cloth were bound tightly around his body from neck to feet, each arm and leg wrapped separately. A cloth was placed over his face. To "loose" Lazarus meant to unbind his arms and legs so that he could move freely.

How many people are living each day like walking dead people! They are bound by anxiety, fears, frustrations, and worries. They have no real freedom of motion. They have no sense of options in their life, no sure sense about the future, and no joy. It's time to get free!

Jesus said, "Therefore do not worry, saying, 'What shall we eat?' or 'What shall we drink?' or 'What shall we wear?' For after all these things the Gentiles seek. For your heavenly Father knows that you need all these things. But seek first the kingdom of God and His righteousness, and all these things shall be added to you. Therefore do not worry about tomorrow, for tomorrow will worry about its own things. Sufficient for the day is its own trouble" (Matthew 6:31–34 NKJV).

How is it that we can keep from worry and fear?

The apostle Paul wrote, "Rejoice in the Lord always. Again I will say, rejoice! …Be anxious for nothing, but in everything by prayer and supplication, with thanksgiving, let your requests be made known to God; and the peace of God, which surpasses all understanding, will guard your hearts and minds through Christ Jesus" (Philippians 4:4, 6–7 NKJV).

The psalmist said this, "Enter into His gates with thanksgiving, and into His courts with praise. Be thankful to Him, and bless His name. For the LORD is good; His mercy is everlasting, and His truth endures to all generations" (Psalm 100:4–5 NKJV).

In both of these passages from God's Word, we are told to voice our thanks to the Lord for what He has done and is doing in our lives. We are told to praise the Lord for who He is, has always been, and will always be.

*Praise and thanksgiving can set a person free of anxiety and fear!*

Something wonderful and powerful happens when a person gives abundant thanks and praise to the Lord. It is as if God grows even more powerful, more wise, more loving, and more majestic in our eyes—we see Him as being far greater than any problem we have or need we face. We see Him as being in control of all things in our lives and in our world. Now, God certainly is far beyond our full comprehension when it comes to the *fullness* of His power, wisdom, and glory—we can never thank Him fully or praise Him fully because we can never grasp fully all who God is. But...thanks and praise open something up in us so that we have a growing awareness of God's presence and power. It is that awareness in us that fuels our faith to believe God for help, answers, and miracles. It is that awareness that gives us comfort. And it is that awareness that helps us STOP worrying, STOP feeling anxious or fearful, and STOP feeling overwhelmed by life or stressed out. Thanks and praise create confidence, relaxation, and peace within us. Thanks and praise renew our hope.

Spend more time thanking and praising God. Thank and praise Him throughout any day, for things both great and small. Voice your thanks and praise out loud.

I believe that your day will not only go better, but that deep inside, your spirit will be refreshed.

> *Stress isn't just uncomfortable—*
> *it's disease-producing and can be deadly.*
> *Don't accommodate stress. Get rid of it!*

THE
# ten
COMMANDMENTS
*of Health & Wellness*

REST DEEPLY • REST DEEPLY

REST DEEPLY • REST DEEPLY •

# *Commandment 8*

## SLEEP LONGER
## *and Deeper*

*"Your body needs long, deep hours of sleep to rejuvenate energy and rebuild tissues."*

*COACH*
DODD:

## *Sleep* Is a Necessity for *Good Health*

We live in a nation where the majority of people on any given day admit to being sleep-deprived. The result is costly in many ways. Not only do sleep-deprived people do less work of lesser quality, but they make more errors and have more job-related and transportation-related accidents. Over time, sleep-deprived people have more stress-induced diseases, are more prone to infectious diseases, and have more injuries caused by both work and home-related accidents.

Sleep-deprived people heal slower than people who get sufficient sleep. The absentee rate for workers who are sleep-deprived is much higher than for those who are sleep-satisfied.

Sleep is God's plan, not man's invention. Some people seem to pride themselves on needing very little sleep. In truth, they are creating deep internal stress for their bodies with their lack of sleep, and, over time, they can exhaust their adrenal system and open themselves up to serious health problems. Sleeping is not rooted in laziness or sloth. To the contrary, it is God's method for helping a person maintain optimal health.

Sleep is when the body restores itself. It is when the body's bone and muscle tissues are rebuilt, when cells are replaced, and when hormonal levels are restored to optimal levels. Sleep is also a time when the brain seems to sort information and produce "memory." Many people report that some of their best and most creative ideas come after a good night of sleep.

How much sleep does a person need? The medical research tells us that we need between seven and nine hours of sleep—in sleep terms, at least five full REM cycles, which means that the body falls asleep at a "deep" level that truly produces health benefits. A REM cycle normally is ninety minutes.

If you are not getting that much sleep per night, *on average*, then you need to take steps to get more sleep.

Make a plan to get to bed a half-hour earlier each night this week, and then next week make a plan to get to bed another half-hour earlier—and do this increased sleep adjustment each week until you are getting seven to nine hours of sleep at night. How can you tell the right amount for your body? You should awaken feeling refreshed, eager to face your day, and, ideally, awaken without the need for a wake-up alarm. Everybody's need for sleep varies slightly according to their physical condition. If you need a nap during the day, take one. For the most part, you should develop your level of health so that you have sufficient energy to make it through an entire day without a nap, but *as* you develop greater health, you may find it beneficial to take a twenty-to-forty-minute nap occasionally to renew your energy.

What can you do to help get the sleep you need?

*First, begin to create a quieter atmosphere in your home a couple of hours before bedtime.* Turn the lights a little lower, play soothing music, turn off the television set or computer, and stop dealing actively with work projects, homework, or tasks that demand mental energy. Take a hot soothing bath. Light an aromatherapy candle. Read material that inspires you but doesn't overly excite you to feel strong emotions of anxiety or fear. Spend time in prayer.

*If you are not getting seven to nine hours of sleep a night, on average, your body is sleep-deprived. Take steps to get more sleep.*

*Second, make your last meal of the day an hour or so before bedtime.* Avoid overly spicy foods and overeating. The health plan in this book calls for your last "meal" to be a protein shake or snack. The protein will help you maintain even blood sugar through the night. Many people who awaken at four o'clock in the morning, or close to that time, awaken because their body is wanting fuel. A protein meal an hour before bedtime can often help a person sleep through the night. Also avoid drinking large quantities of any fluid an hour before bedtime and especially avoid drinking caffeinated beverages or other beverages that are stimulants.

*Third, don't exercise right before going to bed.* Finish your exercise routine at least two hours before bedtime. Exercise actually "awakens" the body. You need time to cool down and relax after a workout before sleeping.

*Fourth, create a sleep area that is truly helpful to sleep.* Make sure you have a good mattress and pillow. Your body should be well-supported as you sleep. Invest in sound-deadening materials, either in the form of draperies or fabric hanging, and light-blocking shades or drapes. Your bedroom should be *dark*. If you need to use eyeshades to create a dark environment, do so. If you live in a noisy apartment building or neighborhood, you may find it helpful to have a source of "white noise" or to play a recording of soothing nature sounds or wear soft earplugs. Turn the thermostat down so you are sleeping in a slightly cool atmosphere, but with enough bed covers to keep you warm. Avoid doing anything that is unrelated to sleep in your bedroom, apart from sexual activity if you are married.

*Fifth, insist that your children sleep in their own beds.* While it may be comforting to your child and reassuring to you as a parent to have a young child sleep with you, your child will sleep better, and both you and your spouse will also sleep better, if your child learns to sleep in his own bed.

*Finally, avoid using drugs and medicines to help you either stay awake or fall asleep.* Melatonin is a natural substance that many people find helpful for sleep, but it is best used for limited time periods. Various herbal teas also help promote sleep and produce relaxation effects.

If you are taking diuretics under a physician's order, you may want to talk to your physician about the time of day you take this medication. Taking it right before bedtime may be the reason you find you are getting up multiple times in the night.

The good news is that if you are keeping the commandments already presented about exercise and balanced nutrition, you are already doing a great deal to promote sound sleep. Body conditioning, walking, and stretching exercises, regardless of the time of day of the workout, all help a person sleep better. Good nutrition in moderate portion sizes over six meals a day provides an optimal blood sugar level for sound sleep. Deep breathing before bedtime can also help promote sleep.

### *Sweet Sleep* Is God's Gift

The psalmist says that God "gives His beloved sleep" (Psalm 127:2). In Proverbs we read a wonderful passage that tells us the benefits of "sound wisdom and discretion":

> "They will be life to your soul and grace to your neck. Then you will walk safely in your way, and your foot will not stumble. When you lie down, you will not be afraid; yes, you will lie down and your sleep will be sweet" (Proverbs 3:22–24 NKJV).

What is the spiritual key to a good night's sleep? It is to rest completely in the Lord, trusting God to be your confidence, your guardian, your provider, and your protector at all times and in all situations. That's the way a baby trusts a loving parent. And we all know, babies who are loved and held gently as they sleep seem to be able to sleep just about anywhere and through just about any circumstance! Place yourself in God's everlasting arms every night—visualize Him holding you and gently rocking you to sleep—and you likely will experience sweet sleep.

How many times do we stay awake worrying, mulling over what might happen and projecting all of the "what if" scenarios we are capable of imagining? How often do we stay awake fantasizing about what "might be" and secretly devising ways to do things that we know are not God's best for us? How often do we stay awake out of fear or as a result of feeling "hurt" over the insults, rejection, or criticism hurled at us during the previous day?

If you find yourself awake for any of these reasons, there's a simple spiritual remedy: PRAY!

## "Vision is the art of seeing things invisible."

Prayer is talking to God, and, specifically, prayer is making requests of God. Spend some time in thanksgiving and praise, and then talk to God about your problems, fears, hurts, anxieties, and desires. Ask God to heal you, restore you, help you, defend you, and to forgive you for those things you may have done to contribute to your own pain and sorrow. Ask God to resolve all things for your good. And then give all of the good and the bad of the previous day over to God in your heart and ask God to help you sleep.

We must check our own hearts to make sure our motives in asking are right before God, but then God's Word tells us to be bold in asking God for what we need and desire (James

4:2–3). After we ask, we must cast ourselves completely on God's care, as God's Word tells us to do: "Humble yourselves under the mighty hand of God, that He may exalt you in due time, casting all your care upon Him, for He cares for you" (1 Peter 5:6–7 NKJV). To "humble yourself" means that you simply put yourself under the hand of God, allowing Him to shield you, comfort you, and protect you as He acts on your behalf. We must begin to anticipate and expect God's answers, knowing that He will raise us up in greater health and wholeness emotionally, spiritually, and physically in His timing.

*Visualize yourself being rocked in God's everlasting arms and you likely will experience sweet sleep.*

Pray...and then trust God to work on your behalf and to answer your prayers according to His methods, His timing, and, ultimately, for your eternal benefit and His glory.

**Focus on God's Goodness.** As part of your prayer time with the Lord, focus on the goodness of God and on the many ways in which He has protected you and provided for you in the past. The apostle Paul wrote to the Philippians that they should meditate—which means to contemplate, consider, focus their minds—upon things that are noble, just, pure, lovely, of good report, virtuous, and praiseworthy. Take authority over your own thoughts and simply *refuse* to return to worry, fear, or feelings of hurt after you have voiced your petitions to God. Let go of the old thoughts associated with your pain, frustrations, and disappointments, and choose to think new thoughts of God's goodness, greatness, and the many ways in which He has brought blessings into your life.

Proverbs 3:5–6 tells us:

"Trust in the LORD with all your heart,
And lean not on your own understanding;
In all your ways acknowledge Him,
And He shall direct your paths."

Begin to expect God to direct your paths from the moment you wake up tomorrow morning. Expect Him to give you a better day, a brighter future, a more fulfilled life, a bigger blessing, an enlarged purpose, and a heart that is healed and capable of loving fully once again.

*Ask God to use your sleeping hours to implant*
*HIS creative ideas, HIS loving attitude,*
*and HIS dreams for you into your heart.*

# THE
# ten
## COMMANDMENTS
*of Health & Wellness*

# *Commandment 9*

## SUPPLEMENT WHAT'S
## *Still Needed*

*"Fill in the gaps."*

## There Are No *Magic Bullets*

There are no magic bullets for good health—no pills or procedures that immediately create health. There *are* good health practices, good exercise routines, good sleep and stress-reducing techniques, and good nutrients. In the end, we do the best we know to do and trust God to do what only He can do.

In the area of nutrition especially, we need to recognize that every person's body is a unique creation of God. We all have slightly different nutritional needs, and we need varying amounts of certain nutrients for optimal health. We also must recognize that our soil and food-production processes today give us foods that are not as rich in minerals and vitamins as foods once were. As much as possible, I suggest that you eat organically grown fruits and vegetables, eat range-fed meats, and choose whole foods that are without additives, fillers, and preservatives. Even so, you likely need to supplement your eating plan with additional nutrients.

I recommend that every person take a good multivitamin pill every day. In addition, most people needed additional amounts of vitamins B, C, and E. The B vitamins, taken as a whole and in sufficient quantity, help brain function and are helpful in reducing stress. Vitamins C and E are great sources of antioxidants that give added protection to every cell of the body as well as the heart muscle and cardiovascular system.

Essential fatty acids are missing in the diet plan of many people. If you frequently choose the "fish" sources of protein on the health plan offered in this book, you are likely getting sufficient fatty acids, also known in the nutrition world as "omegas." You may want to consider taking supplemental fish oil in capsule form. Other omega oils are found in flaxseed oil, hemp oil, evening primrose oil, and borage oil. These oils discourage fat storage and encourage fat burning.

Many women benefit from taking supplemental calcium to help maintain strong bones. Men can benefit from calcium as well!

People with certain chronic conditions often benefit from specific supplements. Increasingly, the companies that manufacture supplements are gearing various combinations of vitamins, minerals, and even herbs to address specific medical conditions. If you haven't been to a health food or nutrition store in a while, you likely will be amazed at all the products that are now available.

*We all have slightly different nutritional needs, and we need varying amounts of certain nutrients for optimal health.*

There are a number of other supplements that are worthy of your consideration. Talk to a nutrition expert at a health food store or to a physician who has studied nutrition. (Note: Be aware that not all physicians have studied good nutritional practices.)

Elsewhere in this book I have noted the value of certain herbs in promoting sleep and relaxation, the availability of fiber supplements, and I have recommended the use of powdered whey protein. We live in an amazing time—what we aren't able to get through our foods, we *can* get in other forms. Avail yourself of the opportunity that supplements provide to you for greater health.

As an overall word of advice: Choose high-quality supplements from reputable providers. This is especially important if you are dealing with herbs, which often have not been studied scientifically as much as certain vitamins and minerals. Take the lowest recommended amount of a supplement, and, if desired, increase to the maximum recommended amount of that supplement. Do not take more than the recommended amount without consulting a physician. A little of some substances goes a long way.

Be wise in your use of supplements: Supplement when a supplement contributes to your better health; don't supplement if you can get the nutrients, fiber, and protein you need in high-quality food sources.

***Supplement Your Understanding.*** In addition to supplementing various nutrients, I am a strong advocate that you need to continually supplement your *knowledge* about health matters. New research is published daily about medical advances. More and more studies are being published that report the benefits of particular health practices and certain nutrients. Here are just a few recent findings you may find interesting:

- Eating two tablespoons of flaxseed oil a day has been shown to cut the risk of breast cancer in half.

- Eating hot and spicy chili peppers can raise a person's metabolic rate, temporarily stimulating the body to burn fat and sugars.
- Three servings of nuts and seeds per week can help control weight, decrease the risk of cancer, heart disease, and diabetes, and help visibly reduce the signs of aging, such as wrinkles and sagging skin.
- Taking one half tablespoon of glutamine dissolved in water three times a day can help a person maintain a weight-loss program and reduce the occurrence of obesity-related diseases.
- The phytonutrient compounds in cinnamon have beneficial effects on controlling blood sugar. Cinnamon has flavon 3-ol polyphenol-class antioxidants that are similar to those found in grapes, berries, cocoa, and green tea. Try sprinkling a little cinnamon on your pancakes and protein shakes!

## "To lose patience is to lose the battle."

You obviously can't read everything available, but you can do a great deal to become better informed about your body and how it works...about your mind and how it works...and about how your body and mind work together. Ask God for wisdom in helping you get to the most useful and reliable, tested-and-proven information available, and then to show you ways in which to apply that information to your life.

## The Church Is for *EVERY Person*

From time to time, I meet people who tell me that they don't go to church, and when they admit that to me, they often add, "I'm a very spiritual person. I just don't go to church." In other words, they don't think they *need* to go to church.

They are wrong.

Every person needs to be part of a community of people who believe in Jesus Christ as their Savior and are seeking to follow Jesus Christ as their Lord. Every person needs to be where he can hear Bible-based preaching and teaching that is presented in a balanced, full, and Christ-exalting way. Every person needs to be where the anointing of the Holy Spirit is flowing freely, and where the gifts of the Spirit are being manifested. Every person needs to be able to join with other believers in prayer, in praise and thanksgiving, and in service to those who are lost spiritually or in need of any kind. Every person needs to experience the love and support of godly friends who offer godly encouragement and, at times, words of exhortation and admonition to be more diligent in obeying God's commands.

*You need what a good church can give to you. And that church needs what you can give to it.*

God did not design us to "go it alone" when it comes to following Jesus or fulfilling the work that the Lord calls us to do. We need one another, and the Word of God tells us plainly that we are not to forsake, or neglect, times of fellowship with other believers in Christ Jesus (Hebrews 10:25).

In many ways, the "gaps" we have in our lives are filled by other Christians around us. At times, we do not see our own sins, errors, our own flaws. Even more often, I believe, we do not see the gifts and areas of strengths that God has given to us or is building within us. We need others to teach us, guide us, encourage us, and support us, not only in their words but by the living examples of their lives. In turn, we benefit greatly by giving our gifts, ideas, and words of encouragement to them.

Consider also those you know who are not following Jesus as their Savior and Lord. As you witness to those people, keep in mind that you can't be everything to every person who needs God. You can't answer every question, meet every need, or fulfill God's ministry call in another person's life. You need to bring the lost to Christ and do so in the context of a church, so that the person you win can be adequately taught and encouraged to become not only a believer but a genuine disciple (follower) of Christ.

Not every person has the same spiritual gifts (see 1 Corinthians 12:4–11 and Romans 12:3–8). Not every person fills all the roles in a church. The apostle Paul wrote in Ephesians 4:11–15 NKJV:

> "He Himself gave some to be apostles, some prophets, some evangelists, and some pastors and teachers, for the equipping of the saints for the work of ministry,

for the edifying of the body of Christ, till we all come to the unity of the faith and of the knowledge of the Son of God, to a perfect man, to the measure of the stature of the fullness of Christ; that we should no longer be children, tossed to and fro and carried about with every wind of doctrine, by the trickery of men, in the cunning craftiness of deceitful plotting, but, speaking the truth in love, may grow up in all things into Him who is the head."

You need what a good church can give to you. And that church needs what you can give to it. Ask God to lead you to the place where you can both receive greatly and give greatly. Then get involved and stay involved.

The church is God's "supplement plan" for every Christian.

*Identify what you need "more of" in your physical and spiritual life. And then ask God to show you where His abundant supply is available!*

THE
# ten
COMMANDMENTS
*of Health & Wellness*

STAY BALANCED • STAY BAL

# Commandment 10

## LIVE IN
## *Balance*

*"Life has rhythms and seasons.
Stay in harmony with them even
as you develop consistent habits
and unwavering faith and character."*

COACH
DODD:

## A *Healthy Person* Is a *Balanced Person*

Every automobile driver knows what it means to drive with unbalanced tires. Not only is the ride bumpy, but the car tends to veer to the left or right, and, over time, the tires wear unevenly and are more prone to blowouts.

The same is true in a person's life. We are both physical and spiritual beings. Some things we do alone, and other things we are better to do as couples, teams, or groups. Some things require effort and exertion, and other things require rest and recreation. Our challenge is to find *balance.*

Many people seem to struggle in maintaining a balance between work and play and between obligations to others and obligations to self. What I know as a personal trainer to some of the top people in their respective professions is this:

The pursuit of better health and the keeping of the 10 Commandments of Health and Wellness we have presented in this book may *seem* like an individual, rather self-centered pursuit. But in the end, other people benefit. The healthier you are, and the more balanced a life you lead, the more your family members will benefit—not only by your better attitude and strength, but by your example that shows your children *how* to be healthy and to become the best they can be for God.

I also know that the healthier you are and the more balanced your life, the more you will have a sense of total well-being. You likely will feel that the quality of your life is rising. Your work will be more creative and easier, your attitude will be more positive, and your relationships will be more relaxed and loving. When that happens, virtually *everything* in your life—both tasks and relationships—is impacted in a positive and beneficial way.

Wholeness is the opposite of disease, fragmentation, and uncompensated weakness. Wholeness bears the marks of strength, harmony, energy, and a vibrancy about all of life. Seek to be whole.

Nothing about the seven-week health plan calls for you to become a "health nut," a "fitness fanatic," or to dive off the cliff into a radical lifestyle. The health plan works for people of all ages and both sexes. It is a plan that can become a way of living.

I truly believe you can have a life of abundant health. I encourage you to pursue such a life and don't settle for anything less.

## Seek a *Consistency* That Transcends *Circumstance*

The writer of the Book of Ecclesiastes said this:

"To everything there is a season,
a time for every purpose under heaven:
A time to be born, and a time to die.
A time to plant, and a time to pluck what is planted...

A time to break down, and a time to build up...

A time to cast away stones [dismantle], and a time to gather stones [build]...

A time to gain, and a time to lose...." (3:1–3, 5–6 NKJV)

Life has rhythms and cycles. It has ebbs and flows. It has good times and bad. At times we need to be more concerned about one area of our lives, and at times other areas. At times we need to throw ourselves wholeheartedly into a project or task, and at other times we need to step back and reevaluate what we are doing.

"The difference between an unsuccessful person and others is not the lack of strength, not the lack of knowledge, but a lack of will."—Vince Lombardi

Now is the time for you to make a decision. I hope you will decide to do Dodd's "Seven-Week Health Plan." I have. It worked for me.

Even so, as a part of life's ebbs and flows, you'll find these things true in your spiritual life and in your developing relationship with Christ Jesus:

There are times for learning...and times for applying what you've learned to real-life situations.

There are times for receiving...and times for giving.

There are times for engaging in intense prayer and spiritual warfare...and there are times for quietly trusting God with steadfast faith that He is working behind the scenes to turn all things for good.

There are times to speak up...and times to keep quiet.

There are times to reach out to people...and times to reflect quietly alone on matters related to your personal and private life.

At no time, however, are we to give in to circumstances and allow life's "times" to dictate our character or our faith. God calls us spiritually to a consistency that transcends all circumstances.

In the midst of life's ebbs and flows, God calls His people to be faithful in their relationship with Him. There is NEVER a time when we are wise to conclude, "This is a time I can disobey, or this is a time when it's acceptable to become lukewarm in my relationship with God, or this is a time when I can stop reading my Bible, or this is a time to walk away from the church."

At ALL times we are challenged by God's Word to love God with our whole heart, mind, and strength, and to love others as ourselves. There must be no ebb or flow in our commitment to the Lord. There must be no wavering in our faith or in our desire to obey the Lord to the best of our ability.

A balanced life is a steadfast, faithful life, and, because it is, it is always a life that is on an upward track. The balanced Christian life is a life that is ever drawing closer to God and closer to heaven.

As part of the Seven-Week Health Plan, I've added to each day the exact same words of advice:

• Spend time in prayer, praise, and thanksgiving.
• Spend time reading the Word of God.

• Spend time loving another person in the Name of Jesus.

How much time you spend in prayer and in reading God's Word is up to you. The ways in which you express genuine Christian love to another person is also up to you. I trust you to give a QUANTITY of high-QUALITY time to the development of your own spiritual life.

On Sundays, I'm advising you to go to church.

There are other spiritual disciplines that are important. When it comes to attending Bible study or helping with an outreach ministry, I trust you to write in that spiritual activity on the days that are appropriate to your individual schedule.

Consistency matters. Some things in life are worthy of doing *every day*. Today's effort and work creates the foundation for tomorrow's effort and work. Today's prayers build tomorrow's character and faith. Today's habits produce tomorrow's rewards. Today's spiritual disciplines produce spiritual maturity, but only if those disciplines are practiced regularly over time.

Never forget these words of Jesus: "Seek first the kingdom of God and His righteousness, and all these things [you need and desire] will be added to you" (Matthew 6:33 NKJV).

God is the author of everything that produces health and balance. Seek Him as your first priority and trust Him to make you whole.

*A balanced pursuit of all that is healthful*
*and good is pleasing to God.*
*A healthy life is a gift from God.*

# THE
# ten
## COMMANDMENTS
*of Health & Wellness*

## THE SEVEN-WEEK
# *Health Plan*

*IN ANTICIPATION* (several days before you begin)

Take your measurements and "before pictures."

Clean any food items from your home that are not on the approved lists.

Go to the grocery store and restock your kitchen with enough good food to last through the first week.

## Day 1 *(start on a Monday)*

- Do the 24-Hour Cleanse described as part of Commandment 5.
- Set your alarm clock for an hour earlier than usual so you can go for a morning walk before work or school.
- Go to bed in sufficient time to get 7 to 9 hours of sleep.

*Spiritually:*

- Spend time in prayer, praise, and thanksgiving.
- Spend time reading the Word of God.
- Spend time loving another person in the Name of Jesus.

## Day 2

- Follow Meal Plan L
- Stretching Exercises
- Walk 7/7 = 14 minutes total

*Spiritually:*

- Spend time in prayer, praise, and thanksgiving.
- Spend time reading the Word of God.
- Spend time loving another person in the Name of Jesus.

## Day 3

- Follow Meal Plan M
- Total Body Conditioning Workout

*Spiritually:*

- Spend time in prayer, praise, and thanksgiving.
- Spend time reading the Word of God.
- Spend time loving another person in the Name of Jesus.

## Day 4

- Follow Meal Plan M
- Stretching Exercises
- Walk 7/7 = 14 minutes total
- *Encouragement from the Coach:* You may be a little stiff or sore today. This is normal. Work hard today because tomorrow you have a full day of rest.

*Spiritually:*
- Spend time in prayer, praise, and thanksgiving.
- Spend time reading the Word of God.
- Spend time loving another person in the Name of Jesus.

## Day 5

- Follow Meal Plan M
- (no exercise—a day of rest)
- *Encouragement from the Coach:* Let your body recover from your workouts this week. Enjoy your accomplishments and anticipate a blessed weekend!

*Spiritually:*
- Spend time in prayer, praise, and thanksgiving.
- Spend time reading the Word of God.
- Spend time loving another person in the Name of Jesus.

## Day 6

- Follow Meal Plan H
- Full Body Conditioning Workout
- *Encouragement from the Coach:* Today is a workout day, but also a heavy complex-carb day—not a bad day at all! Put up a few motivational scriptures and quotes where you are likely to read and see them daily. YOU are the best motivator of YOU.

*Spiritually:*
- Spend time in prayer, praise, and thanksgiving.
- Spend time reading the Word of God.
- Spend time loving another person in the Name of Jesus.

## Day 7

- Follow Meal Plan H
- (no exercise—a day of rest)

*Spiritually:*
- Spend time in prayer, praise, and thanksgiving.
- Spend time reading the Word of God.
- Spend time loving another person in the Name of Jesus.
- GO TO CHURCH

*Week TWO*

## Day 8

- Follow Meal Plan N
- Stretching Exercises
- Walk 10.5/10.5 = 21 minutes total
- *Encouragement from the Coach:* Walking gets a little tougher today as we add more time. This is your first no complex-carb day, but you'll likely discover that it isn't hard.

*Spiritually:*
- Spend time in prayer, praise, and thanksgiving.
- Spend time reading the Word of God.
- Spend time loving another person in the Name of Jesus.

## Day 9

- Follow Meal Plan L
- Total Body Conditioning Exercises
- *Encouragement from the Coach:* You get to add some complex carbs today!

*Spiritually:*
- Spend time in prayer, praise, and thanksgiving.
- Spend time reading the Word of God.
- Spend time loving another person in the Name of Jesus.

## Day 10

- Follow Meal Plan M
- Stretching Exercises
- Walk 10.5/10.5 = 21 minutes total
- *Encouragement from the Coach:* If you don't already have a walking partner, call a friend and recruit a walking partner. You'll enjoy your walks even more.

*Spiritually:*
- Spend time in prayer, praise, and thanksgiving.
- Spend time reading the Word of God.
- Spend time loving another person in the Name of Jesus.

## Day 11

- Follow Meal Plan M

- (no exercise—a day of rest)
- *Encouragement from the Coach:* Today is a total rest day and also a moderate complex-carb day. Enjoy! Rest up for tomorrow!

*Spiritually:*
- Spend time in prayer, praise, and thanksgiving.
- Spend time reading the Word of God.
- Spend time loving another person in the Name of Jesus.

## Day 12

- Follow Meal Plan L
- Total Body Conditioning Workout
- *Encouragement from the Coach:* Muscles are the only place where the body burns fuel—namely, fat and carbohydrates. That's why a good workout program is so important.

*Spiritually:*
- Spend time in prayer, praise, and thanksgiving.
- Spend time reading the Word of God.
- Spend time loving another person in the Name of Jesus.

## Day 13

- Follow Meal Plan H
- Stretching Exercises
- Walk 14/14 = 28 minutes total

*Spiritually:*
- Spend time in prayer, praise, and thanksgiving.
- Spend time reading the Word of God.
- Spend time loving another person in the Name of Jesus.

## Day 14

- Follow Meal Plan H
- (no exercise—a day of rest)

*Spiritually:*
- Spend time in prayer, praise, and thanksgiving.
- Spend time reading the Word of God.
- Spend time loving another person in the Name of Jesus.
- GO TO CHURCH

## Day 15

- Follow Meal Plan N
- Total Body Conditioning Workout
- *Encouragement from the Coach:* Keep up the good work! You've finished two full weeks of the plan and are starting your third week!

*Spiritually:*
- Spend time in prayer, praise, and thanksgiving.
- Spend time reading the Word of God.
- Spend time loving another person in the Name of Jesus.

## Day 16

- Follow Meal Plan L
- Stretching Exercises
- Walk 14/14 = 28 minutes total

*Spiritually:*
- Spend time in prayer, praise, and thanksgiving.
- Spend time reading the Word of God.
- Spend time loving another person in the Name of Jesus.

## Day 17

- Follow Meal Plan M
- Total Body Conditioning Workout
- *Encouragement from the Coach:* This is your sixth total body workout. By now you should know the routine fairly well. Try to increase your repetitions on all the exercises.

*Spiritually:*
- Spend time in prayer, praise, and thanksgiving.
- Spend time reading the Word of God.
- Spend time loving another person in the Name of Jesus.

## Day 18

- Follow Meal Plan M
- (no exercise—a total of rest)
- *Encouragement from the Coach:* You worked hard

yesterday, especially if you increased your reps for all the exercises. Enjoy a day of rest!

*Spiritually:*

- Spend time in prayer, praise, and thanksgiving.
- Spend time reading the Word of God.
- Spend time loving another person in the Name of Jesus.

## Day 19

- Follow Meal Plan L
- Stretching Exercises
- Walk 17.5/17.5 = 35 minutes total
- *Encouragement from the Coach:* Time was added to your walk today…but I know you can do it!

*Spiritually:*

- Spend time in prayer, praise, and thanksgiving.
- Spend time reading the Word of God.
- Spend time loving another person in the Name of Jesus.

## Day 20

- Follow Meal Plan H
- Total Body Conditioning Workout

*Spiritually:*

- Spend time in prayer, praise, and thanksgiving.
- Spend time reading the Word of God.
- Spend time loving another person in the Name of Jesus.

## Day 21

- Follow Meal Plan H
- (no exercise—a day of rest)
- *Encouragement from the Coach:* You've completed three weeks! Have a blessed and relaxing day.

*Spiritually:*

- Spend time in prayer, praise, and thanksgiving.
- Spend time reading the Word of God.
- Spend time loving another person in the Name of Jesus.
- GO TO CHURCH

## Day 22

- Follow Meal Plan N
- Stretching Exercises
- Walk 17.5/17.5 = 35 minutes total
- *Encouragement from the Coach:* Try to go a little bit farther on each stretch. Take your time. Stay strong!

*Spiritually:*
- Spend time in prayer, praise, and thanksgiving.
- Spend time reading the Word of God.
- Spend time loving another person in the Name of Jesus.

## Day 23

- Follow Meal Plan N
- Total Body Conditioning Workout
- *Encouragement from the Coach:* Today's workout may have seemed a little tougher since you didn't have any complex carbs yesterday and no complex carbs today. This is the first time you've gone two days without complex carbs, but I know you can survive this!

*Spiritually:*
- Spend time in prayer, praise, and thanksgiving.
- Spend time reading the Word of God.
- Spend time loving another person in the Name of Jesus.

## Day 24

- Follow Meal Plan L
- Stretching Exercises
- Walk 21/21 = 42 minutes total
- *Encouragement from the Coach:* The good news is that you have complex carbohydates today. The bad news is that you have a walk that's seven minutes longer. Stay with the program. You can do it!

*Spiritually:*
- Spend time in prayer, praise, and thanksgiving.
- Spend time reading the Word of God.
- Spend time loving another person in the Name of Jesus.

## Day 25

- Follow Meal Plan M
- (no exercise—a day of rest)
- *Encouragement from the Coach:* Your last three days were the toughest so far. You deserve the good rest of today! Take heart—you just crossed the halfway mark in the program!

*Spiritually:*
- Spend time in prayer, praise, and thanksgiving.
- Spend time reading the Word of God.
- Spend time loving another person in the Name of Jesus.

## Day 26

- Follow Meal Plan M
- Total Body Conditioning Workout

*Spiritually:*
- Spend time in prayer, praise, and thanksgiving.
- Spend time reading the Word of God.
- Spend time loving another person in the Name of Jesus.

## Day 27

- Follow Meal Plan H
- Stretching Exercises
- Walk 21/21 = 42 minutes total
- *Encouragement from the Coach:* Enjoy the carbs!

*Spiritually:*
- Spend time in prayer, praise, and thanksgiving.
- Spend time reading the Word of God.
- Spend time loving another person in the Name of Jesus.

## Day 28

- Follow Meal Plan H
- (no exercise—a day of rest)
- *Encouragement from the Coach:* Enjoy a great day of rest and relaxation. You'll need it—we shift into high gear tomorrow. Prepare for fitness warfare. The next 21 days are going to produce incredible results!

*Spiritually:*
- Spend time in prayer, praise, and thanksgiving.
- Spend time reading the Word of God.
- Spend time loving another person in the Name of Jesus.
- GO TO CHURCH

## Day 29

- Follow Meal Plan A
- Total Body Conditioning Workout
- *Encouragement from the Coach:* The next three weeks are going to be the most gratifying weeks. Day by day you are going to see transformation!

*Spiritually:*
- Spend time in prayer, praise, and thanksgiving.
- Spend time reading the Word of God.
- Spend time loving another person in the Name of Jesus.

## Day 30

- Follow Meal Plan A
- Stretching Exercise
- Walk 24.5/24.5 = 49 minutes total

*Spiritually:*
- Spend time in prayer, praise, and thanksgiving.
- Spend time reading the Word of God.
- Spend time loving another person in the Name of Jesus.

## Day 31

- Follow Meal Plan A
- Total Body Conditioning Workout
- *Encouragement from the Coach:* Work out HARD. Enjoy the way you are feeling. Enjoy the fact that your workout is making your bones strong and your body lean.

*Spiritually:*
- Spend time in prayer, praise, and thanksgiving.
- Spend time reading the Word of God.
- Spend time loving another person in the Name of Jesus.

## Day 32

- Follow Meal Plan B
- (no exercise—a day of rest)
- *Encouragement from the Coach:* Refuse to be defeated.

You may win at times, and you may lose at times, but you don't ever need to be DEFEATED.

*Spiritually:*
- Spend time in prayer, praise, and thanksgiving.
- Spend time reading the Word of God.
- Spend time loving another person in the Name of Jesus.

## Day 33

- Follow Meal Plan B
- Stretching Exercises
- Walk 24.5/24.5 = 49 minutes total
- *Encouragement from the Coach:* Don't allow yourself to fall into a slump. Slumps are like a soft bed—easy to collapse into but hard to get out of.

*Spiritually:*
- Spend time in prayer, praise, and thanksgiving.
- Spend time reading the Word of God.
- Spend time loving another person in the Name of Jesus.

## Day 34

- Follow Meal Plan C
- Total Body Conditioning Workout

*Spiritually:*
- Spend time in prayer, praise, and thanksgiving.
- Spend time reading the Word of God.
- Spend time loving another person in the Name of Jesus.

## Day 35

- Follow Meal Plan C
- (no exercise—a day of rest)
- *Encouragement from the Coach:* A blessed day! Full body rest and two big complex-carb meals!

*Spiritually:*
- Spend time in prayer, praise, and thanksgiving.
- Spend time reading the Word of God.
- Spend time loving another person in the Name of Jesus.
- GO TO CHURCH

## Day 36

- Follow Meal Plan B
- Stretching Exercises
- Walk 28/28 = 56 minutes total
- *Encouragement from the Coach:* Congratulations—you are entering the home stretch. Your body is looking better and better.

*Spiritually:*
- Spend time in prayer, praise, and thanksgiving.
- Spend time reading the Word of God.
- Spend time loving another person in the Name of Jesus.

## Day 37

- Follow Meal Plan B
- Total Body Conditioning Workout
- *Encouragement from the Coach:* Stay strong! Find good reasons to laugh. Your body will enjoy the release of endorphins (a natural pain killer and a feel-good hormone).

*Spiritually:*
- Spend time in prayer, praise, and thanksgiving.
- Spend time reading the Word of God.
- Spend time loving another person in the Name of Jesus.

## Day 38

- Follow Meal Plan B
- Stretching Exercises
- Walk 28/28 = 56 minutes total
- *Encouragement from the Coach:* Remember to relax as you stretch and to be patient with your stretching routine.

*Spiritually:*
- Spend time in prayer, praise, and thanksgiving.
- Spend time reading the Word of God.
- Spend time loving another person in the Name of Jesus.

## Day 39

- Follow Meal Plan B

- (no exercise—a day of rest)

*Spiritually:*
- Spend time in prayer, praise, and thanksgiving.
- Spend time reading the Word of God.
- Spend time loving another person in the Name of Jesus.

## Day 40

- Follow Meal Plan A
- Total Body Conditioning Workout
- *Encouragement from the Coach:* Celebrate the fact that you are getting closer and closer to victory!

*Spiritually:*
- Spend time in prayer, praise, and thanksgiving.
- Spend time reading the Word of God.
- Spend time loving another person in the Name of Jesus.

## Day 41

- Follow Meal Plan A
- Stretching Exercises
- Walk 35/35 = 70 minutes total
- *Encouragement from the Coach:* This is your biggest exercise day so far. You can handle it!

*Spiritually:*
- Spend time in prayer, praise, and thanksgiving.
- Spend time reading the Word of God.
- Spend time loving another person in the Name of Jesus.

## Day 42

- Follow Meal Plan C
- (no exercise—a day of rest)
- *Encouragement from the Coach:* Another blessed Sunday. Rest and prepare yourself mentally for your biggest week—your final week of the plan!

*Spiritually:*
- Spend time in prayer, praise, and thanksgiving.
- Spend time reading the Word of God.
- Spend time loving another person in the Name of Jesus.
- GO TO CHURCH

## Day 43

---

- Follow Meal Plan B
- Total Body Conditioning Workout
- *Encouragement from the Coach:* Look at yourself in a mirror and tell yourself, "Nothing can stop me now!"

*Spiritually:*
- Spend time in prayer, praise, and thanksgiving.
- Spend time reading the Word of God.
- Spend time loving another person in the Name of Jesus.

## Day 44

---

- Follow Meal Plan B
- Stretching Exercises
- Walk 35/35 = 70 minutes total
- *Encouragement from the Coach:* A tough day, but you know by now that you can handle tough days!

*Spiritually:*
- Spend time in prayer, praise, and thanksgiving.
- Spend time reading the Word of God.
- Spend time loving another person in the Name of Jesus.

## Day 45

---

- Follow Meal Plan B
- Total Body Conditioning Workout
- *Encouragement from the Coach:* Give everything you've got to your workout—tomorrow is a rest day!

*Spiritually:*
- Spend time in prayer, praise, and thanksgiving.
- Spend time reading the Word of God.
- Spend time loving another person in the Name of Jesus.

## Day 46

---

- Follow Meal Plan B
- (no exercise—a day of rest)

• *Encouragement from the Coach:* ENJOY the rest. Only a few days to go!

*Spiritually:*
- Spend time in prayer, praise, and thanksgiving.
- Spend time reading the Word of God.
- Spend time loving another person in the Name of Jesus.

## Day 47

- Follow Meal Plan B
- Stretching Exercises
- Walk 35/35 = 70 minutes total

• *Encouragement from the Coach:* Prepare yourself mentally and physically for a tough day tomorrow—get a little more sleep tonight.

*Spiritually:*
- Spend time in prayer, praise, and thanksgiving.
- Spend time reading the Word of God.
- Spend time loving another person in the Name of Jesus.

## Day 48

- Follow Meal Plan C
- Stretching Exercises
- Total Body Conditioning Workout
- Walk 38.5/38.5 = 77 minutes

• *Encouragement from the Coach:* That's right! All three types of exercises in one day! Afterward, enjoy a delicious Plan-C carbs meal! Be proud of yourself. I'm proud of you for making the commitment and sticking with the plan!

*Spiritually:*
- Spend time in prayer, praise, and thanksgiving.
- Spend time reading the Word of God.
- Spend time loving another person in the Name of Jesus.

## Day 49

- Follow Meal Plan C
- (no exercise—a day of rest)

• Take your measurements and compare to your "before" measurements.

• Take a new photograph to compare with your "before" picture.

• Celebrate the spiritual warrior you are!

• *Encouragement from the Coach:* Congratulations! You have accomplished something that few have the heart or discipline to do! Enjoy a total rest day. Enjoy each meal. Celebrate your accomplishment in a godly way!

*Spiritually:*
• Spend time in prayer, praise, and thanksgiving.
• Spend time reading the Word of God.
• Spend time loving another person in the Name of Jesus.
• GO TO CHURCH
• Read 2 Timothy 4:7 aloud to yourself: "I have fought the good fight. I have finished the race. I have kept the faith!"

• *Encouragement from Coach Paula:* I'm proud of you, too! What an accomplishment! Praise God! Now…encourage someone else to do what you have done!

# THE ten COMMANDMENTS

*of Health & Wellness*

## *Recipes*

## Hummus

- 1 (15 oz) can of chickpeas (garbanzo beans), drained
- 1/4 cup lemon juice
- 2 cloves garlic, peeled
- 1 tbsp. flaxseed oil
- 1/4 tsp ground cumin

In food processor, combine chickpeas and garlic; mix together the lemon juice, flaxseed oil, and cumin—add to the chickpea and garlic mixture and blend for one minute.

## Protein Pancake

- 5 scoops protein powder (optimum nutrition protein—direct vanilla)
- 3 eggs whites
- water
- Pam® spray

In mixing bowl, combine protein powder and egg whites; add water a little bit at a time until the mixture has the consistency of pancake batter. Spray Pam® on griddle and cook the pancake until light brown on each side.

## Protein Cake and Cupcakes

**(Parillo Hi-Protein Cake and Cupcake Mix)**

*Makes 1 cake or 6 cupcakes*

- 1 cup water
- 3-1/2 tbsp vegetable oil
- 6 level scoops (6 servings) cake mix

Preheat oven to 350 degrees. For toaster oven, set temperature to 350 degrees and preheat 5 minutes before baking.

Mix ingredients thoroughly.

**For cake:** Pour batter into a nonstick cake pan (8"x8" square or an 8" round).

**For cupcakes:** Divide batter evenly into muffin pan lined with full baking cups.

In a conventional oven, bake for 18–20 minutes or until inserted toothpick comes out clean.

In a toaster oven, bake for 10–12 minutes or until inserted toothpick comes out clean.

Over baking will cause dryness.

## Paula White Books

*Birthing Your Dreams*

*Daily Treasures*

*Deal With It!*

*Fasting Made Simple*

*First Fruits: From Promise to Provision*

*He Loves Me, He Loves Me Not*

*I Don't Get Wholeness . . . That's the Problem*

*I Promise You . . .*

*Life by Design Daily Planner*

*Living the Abundant Life*

*Morning by Morning*

*Simple Suggestions for a Sensational Life*

## Paula White Journals

*Conversations With God*

*Dare to Soar*

*Dreamer's*

*Leading a Life of Integrity, Excellence, and Results*

*Men of Honor*

# Notes

# Notes

# Notes

# Notes

## Notes

# Notes

# Notes

# Notes

# Notes